The editor
and contributors . . .

Joseph B. Gittler possesses a insight into the problems of grou lations as the result of extensive ex- perience in the field. Director of the University of Rochester's Center for the Study of Group Relations, he served as chairman of the Institute on Minority Groups in the United States which met in 1955. He is the author of numerous books and papers in soci- ology and is a former editor of *Mid- west Sociologist*.

Dr. Gittler received his undergrad- uate training at the University of Georgia and took his doctorate in sociology from the University of Chi- cago in 1941. He has been on the faculty of the University of Chicago, Iowa State College, the University of Georgia, and Drake University. At present he is professor and chairman of the department of sociology at the University of Rochester.

In addition to editing *Understand- ing Minority Groups,* Dr. Gittler has contributed a chapter bearing the same title.

This . . .
ten auth . . .   d persuasions,
but who . . .   the unfinished
business . . .

In r . . .   wareness that
majority- . . .   ous problems,
stemming . . .   treatment of
minority . . .   societies, has
been clos . . .   ligious affiliation. Thi . . .   s.

The . . .   presented in
lecture f . . .   the United
States, sp . . .   Relations of
the Univ . . .   te clearly revealed th . . .   ciologist, the
historian, . . .   and folly of
discrimin . . .   by those in
attendanc . . .   emancipator,
we are slowly moving toward a reassessment of values and practices.
It was made evident that through a conscientious scrutiny of the
American definitions of freedom, human dignity, and equality, we
can begin to solve the problems of intolerance.

The contributors consider not only the obvious intolerance of
race, color, and creed, but the less often observed intolerance based
upon ignorance, underdevelopment, and stagnation. In this light,
they discuss unequal access to the law, education, and work. Two
unique features of the volume are the chapter on the philosophy and
ethics of group relations and the chapter on understanding minority
groups which sets forth a general framework and posits a number
of principles governing the understanding of all minority groups.

Understanding Minority Groups

Understanding

CONTRIBUTORS

John Collier

Cornelis W. de Kiewiet

Joseph B. Gittler

Theodore H. Haas

Oscar Handlin

John LaFarge, S.J.

Wayne A. R. Leys

Ira de A. Reid

Clarence Senior

Dorothy Swaine Thomas

Minority Groups

JOSEPH B. GITTLER, EDITOR

CHAIRMAN, DEPARTMENT OF SOCIOLOGY

UNIVERSITY OF ROCHESTER

NEW YORK · JOHN WILEY & SONS, INC.

LONDON · CHAPMAN & HALL, LIMITED

To Herman M. Cohn

Preface

In recent years, there has been an increasing awareness that
group relations problems represent one of the basic enigmas of
our time. Of the host of problems stemming from group interaction, that of majority-minority tension is one of the most serious. Minority groups are those groups whose members experience a wide range of discriminatory treatment and frequently are
relegated to positions relatively low in the status structure of our
social system. In American society—as in many others—minority
group status has been closely correlated with specific racial, ethnic,
or religious affiliation. The series of papers presented in this volume deals with six of these minority groups in the United States.

This volume is a compilation of papers presented at the Institute
on Minority Groups in the United States, sponsored by the Center
for the Study of Group Relations of the University of Rochester.
The Institute took place each Monday evening for eight weeks on
the University of Rochester campus, from October 17 through
December 5, 1955. The chapter headings in this book are similar

to the topics of the papers presented at the Institute. Each presentation was followed by three discussants who commented briefly on the paper. The editor regrets that it was impossible to publish the discussions of the papers because of limitations of space. Summaries of these discussions can be obtained from the Center for the Study of Group Relations, Department of Sociology, University of Rochester, Rochester, New York.

I wish to acknowledge with much gratitude the indulgence of the lecturers to the prodding of the editor in readying their papers for publication. The Center for the Study of Group Relations is indeed grateful too, for the contributions of the following discussants to the Institute sessions: Dr. Robert H. Beaven, Dean Lewis W. Beck, Rabbi Philip S. Bernstein, Mr. Kenneth L. Brown, Dr. Hugh C. Burr, Dr. D. Lincoln Canfield, Dr. Vera Micheles Dean, Dr. Peru Farver, Dr. C. Wayne Gordon, Mr. Alfred K. Guthe, Dr. Walter W. Hamburger, Mr. Irving M. Kriegsfeld, Dr. Vincent Nowlis, Father John P. O'Meara, Mr. Charles Otero, Rev. David Owl, Dr. John Romano, Rabbi Stuart E. Rosenberg, Dr. Wilbour Eddy Saunders, Mr. Manheim S. Shapiro, Dr. Paul E. Smith, Mrs. Irving L. Walker, Dr. Ruth Watanabe.

Many thanks are also due the many persons and groups who assisted in the planning and execution of the Institute, to the members of the Sociology staff, to Anne Ludlow, who prepared the manuscripts for publication, and to the following individuals who acted as chairmen of the various sessions: Miss Alice Bacon, Messrs. Clifford E. Carpenter, William Fay, Egil E. Krogh, Sol M. Linowitz, Howard C. Seymour, and Joseph C. Wilson.

And finally, the major burden of both the preparation of this volume and the organization of the Institute has been shared heavily by Lami S. Gittler, whose ceaseless efforts made both possible.

JOSEPH B. GITTLER

January, 1956
Rochester, New York

Introduction

CORNELIS W. DE KIEWIET

The world is still full of the discrimination of race, color, and creed. Some of it lies hidden behind the opaque barriers elevated by communism. In India the discriminations represented by the unequal relationships between the Indian population and the British Raj have disappeared, yet new tensions caused by differences of language and historic tradition have taken their place, so that the wholeness and stability of the new India are not yet firmly assured. In Malaya the status of resident Chinese is menaced by the imminent advent of Malayan self-rule. In Uganda the native population looks with suspicion upon the claim of Indians to the right to hold land or to share in political power. If by some sudden chance Mr. John Foster Dulles' propositions for the emancipation of the Soviet satellites were realized, the Balkans would unquestionably relapse into a bitter debate over the unsettled questions of religion and race, so that Americans would once again have to learn the meaning of Uniate and Greek Orthodox, of Macedonians and Transylvanians.

The ancient compatibility of Jew and Arab has collapsed. South Africa contains the ugliest racial tensions in the modern world. Yet reflective men know that this unpleasant catalog only partially hides the progress the world is making away from intolerance.

Each undergraduate generation takes up the endless debate whether history is a review of progress or merely of change. When the old hatreds pass, but new passions take their place, and when more of the free world is almost each year drawn behind the iron curtain, it becomes hard to speak confidently of progress. Our generation of the hydrogen bomb is closer than even the most chaotic and disturbed of other centuries to understanding the moody eschatological debate that preceded the optimistic teachings of St. Augustine and St. Benedict.

An American college may not always be the best place from which to view the modern world. American education is not more smug or egocentric than British or French education, yet it has these attributes in sufficient degree to have difficulty in seeing the chaos and travail of the modern world through the eyes of, say, almost any delegate to the Bandung Conference. Almost forty years ago General Smuts proclaimed that mankind was on the march. For great masses of the world's population his words are more meaningful today than they were after the First World War. In Asia this perception is clear, militant, and even dangerous; in Africa it is still obscure, sensed rather than seen. To more men than ever before the world seems fuller of opportunities. The words of freedom and emancipation are in the air. Because men are deeply divided on the meaning of freedom and the means of emancipation, part of mankind may be merely on the march to new thralldom. All of mankind may even step into final disaster.

These lectures are not primarily concerned with the great transformations of the modern world. Yet these transformations are an obvious and necessary background. These lectures are the result of an effort to share in the reassessment of the modern world. They are evidence of the conscientiousness of students who recognize that the American definitions of freedom or human dignity or equality are scrutinized from afar. To the extent that they are true or honest they are accepted or rejected. It was no accident

that these lectures were delivered before packed and deeply interested audiences.

The size of the audience and the questions that were asked revealed a clear and conscientious liberalism toward those problems
of race, color, and creed which still exist within American society.
They were, in fact, important evidence of the fact that within
America, too, mankind is on the march. Students of the University of Rochester were part of the slow tide that is evening out
the discrimination of American life. During these lectures, it was
easy to see that it is the scholar, the sociologist, the historian, the
psychologist, and the economist who first expose the error and
folly of discrimination. They prepare the way for the legislator
and the jurist. Scholarship is still the great emancipator.

Entire scholarly careers have been devoted to explaining the rise
of tolerance in the great societies of the western world. Although
simple explanations leave much to be desired, it can be said that
tolerance grows when men recognize that the sum of what they
give to one another is greater than the sum of what they withhold
from one another. The more complex a society becomes and the
greater the range of its economic activities, the greater the degree
of willing cooperation it must have from all elements of its population. A society suffers if laws and conventions impose restric-
tion and inferiority upon any group. One reason why the Jews
of Portugal and Spain were welcome in Holland, even as early as
the sixteenth century, was that Holland's population was not big
enough to carry the burdens of a rapidly growing economy. Holland needed recruits. Modern America, far more than sixteenth
century Holland, is at the stage where she has to insist on drawing
upon her human resources at the highest level. For the older intolerance of race, color, or creed, a new intolerance is being substituted. It is an intolerance of ignorance and underdevelopment
and stagnation. Even in the less enlightened areas of our culture
and economy, it is becoming increasingly clear that unequal access
to the law, education, and work is morally indefensible, economically unprofitable, and politically unwise.

Greatest of all aids in increasing the sum of human cooperation
amongst social groups is a sense of security. The Supreme Court
decision on segregation in education is historically important not

because it was widely and enthusiastically acclaimed, which was not the case, but because the highest court in the land implicitly announced that it was now possible to make a radical declaration of a legal principle without plunging American society into civil strife. This optimistic assumption is now being tested in those parts of the country where the effects of the verdict are most directly felt. Two views are possible. The first is already being exploited by hostile critics of the American scene. It is the view that the power of intolerance and discrimination in America is still considerable. The second is more comforting. It is that the Supreme Court has thrust the issue of educational segregation into the sort of special arena which is characteristic of America's political life. There is no chance now of avoiding the debate and controversy which, even at its noisiest, is part of the American process of self-education and evaluation. How long disagreement and dissension will last is anyone's guess. It can be safely asserted that yet another difficult issue is on the way to improvement.

In a scientific and scholarly sense these essays are part of the debate that will probably go on for the rest of our generation. It is important to note that they contain no simple formulae, and certainly no panaceas or prescriptions. Their importance lies in the comforting fact that men of different persuasions and skills thought it important to work together on this unfinished business of human cooperation.

Contents

Chapter I

The Philosophical and Ethical Aspects of Group Relations

Wayne A. R. Leys

When you are asked about the ethics of intergroup relations, you feel like the backwoods farmer who was asked to direct
a motorist to Nashville. He began confidently, "You take the
south road at the next corner and then turn left. . . . No, you
can't do that: the bridge is out. . . . Well, take the east road. . . .
No, that road is too muddy." The farmer looked out into space
for a minute and then gave the motorist this advice: "Mister, if I
wanted to go to Nashville, I wouldn't start from here."

The *goals* of intergroup friendship and cooperation are very attractive: the elimination of prejudice and hatred. But what are
you going to do about the muddy roads just ahead? What about
the employer who practices racial discrimination? Are you going
to vote for a fair employment practices law? And what about existing restrictions on immigration and intermarriage? And how will
you treat those religious sects that refuse to cooperate with you?
Friendly intergroup relations are prized as an ideal objective, but
the practical next steps are highly controversial.

When people agree on an end and disagree on the means, someone must be ignorant of the means to the end or mistaken about the extent of the agreement on ends. I am going to probe the extent of agreement on ends. In choosing to do so, I know that some of the controversy over such measures as FEPC may stem from ignorance. The current goals and slogans for better human relations date back only one generation. The psychologists and sociologists still have to establish some of the facts and generalizations that are involved in the implementation of the intergroup slogans.[1] But *part* of the difficulty in action programs is a vagueness, if not a hidden conflict, in the ends we seek. Granting that there is still much to be learned about ways and means and methods, I wish to direct attention to the problem of ends.

The consensus which has been felt by participants in the intergroup education movement is not a full agreement on positive goals. It is rather a unanimity in opposing the warmongering totalitarians of the twentieth century. The twentieth century had been expected to produce a peaceful, international civilization. Instead, the century erupted into new tribalisms and a revival of the ideals of war. The Fascists preached international and interracial war, and the Communists preached class struggle.

For a long time the idealists in the western democracies could not believe that the totalitarians meant what they said. Mussolini was regarded as a braggart, a sawdust Caesar who talked war but who actually made the Italian trains run on time. It was not until the Nazis undertook their program of mass murder that we of the West realized that intergroup warfare was being ruthlessly and systematically fostered. It was then that in large numbers we began to join in movements with the opposite purpose of fostering intergroup cooperation. The totalitarians were promoting intergroup conflict. We would promote intergroup friendship.

The Nazis invited a flat contradiction of their purposes, for they stated their belief in war openly and bluntly. War, in their view, was the normal intergroup relationship. Carl Schmitt put the whole ugly business into two sentences:

> The essential political distinction is that between Friend and Foe.
> It gives all human actions and motives their political meaning.[2]

Hitler's orations convinced millions of Germans that the natural political grouping, which determines who is friend and who is foe, is race. Alfred Rosenberg traced the rise and fall of great civilizations and, with specious scholarship, showed the consequence of failure to identify natural enemies. Even in ancient Egypt, Rosenberg found, Aryans had been the creators of civilization, and their downfall came about when they intermarried with inferior races, their natural enemies.[3]

The Nazis repudiated all intergroup moralities, including the Christian ethic of universal love. In 1936 they issued a new "translation" of the Christian gospels in which the reader could not find the beatitude, "Blessed are the peacemakers." According to the translator, Reichsbishop Müller, the correct reading was, "Happy are they who keep peace with their fellow-countrymen." Instead of "Love your enemies," Müller read, "You must be on good terms with your fellow-countrymen and comrades."[4] This twisting of the words of Jesus followed the political theory which the Nazis took over from earlier militarists, viz., that moral obligations traditionally enjoined upon enemies referred only to enemies in private quarrels, not to enemies of the State.

Nazi persecutions and aggressions made the meaning of the Nazi words unmistakable in the thirties. At that time many westerners did not realize that Communism was also a gospel of war. Marx had proclaimed a class struggle and declared that only force could decide whether capitalist or proletarian interests would be served. But there were also some vague Marxist predictions of a happy day when the world would be a peaceful, classless society. The warlike character of Communism had been further obscured by the "revisionist" Marxists, who had abandoned the doctrine of the class struggle, and the Soviet propagandists who periodically announced proposals for disarmament and collective security.

Despite appearances, the Communists were following Lenin, who had kept alive the class war doctrine in his debate with the revisionists way back in 1902. Lenin had at that time called for "revolutionary centralism." Revolutionary centralism was his way of taking seriously the Marxist theory of class warfare. It meant, according to Lenin, a harsh, unscrupulous, conspiratorial discipline with just one immediate objective, namely, the destruction of capitalist power.[5] That war, rather than reform, was the Communist way of life might have been realized earlier and more generally if it had not been disguised by dishonest propaganda. But the propaganda became transparent to more and more outsiders as the party line twisted and turned in the thirties to justify purges, the Russo-Finnish War, and the nonaggression pact with Hitler. In the postwar period Soviet actions revealed Communism as completely devoted to the single objective of victory in a hostile struggle.

I have reviewed the emergence of totalitarianism as the belief in intergroup warfare, because it was, to a large extent, what was being thought about when the various movements for intergroup cooperation developed their slogans. In the thirties the typical ideals of intergroup cooperation were denials of the Nazi creed. In the postwar period, when Soviet practice was widely recognized as similar to Nazi creed, the characteristic beliefs of intergroup educators have been repudiations of all forms of totalitarianism.

The totalitarian philosophy of war can be spelled out in three dogmas. When I mention these dogmas, you will see that the intergroup cooperators have set up their objectives by negating and opposing the totalitarians.

The first dogma of twentieth-century tyranny is the *justification* of war. It declares that persons of different nations, races, or classes cannot understand one another. This is what the totalitarians meant when they talked about ideological barriers. The Nazis said that people with different heredities had completely different understandings of things. The Communists pooh-poohed the Nazi theory of heredity, but they also denied the possibility of intergroup communication. They said that each class has its own ideology, a mass of biases which distort even the science of pure mathematics. Thus, in the Communist view, a person's significant behavior is determined by group membership, and group membership is determined by economic forces. Since economic forces are beyond the individual's control, ideological barriers are as insuperable in the Marxist view as they were in the Nazi view.

The second totalitarian dogma states the *implications* of intergroup warfare *for morality*, viz., there are no universal moral obligations. No human rights transcend the boundaries of class (according to the Communists) or the boundaries of nationality (according to the Fascists). Coercive force must characterize all intergroup relations.

The third totalitarian dogma commands *warlike behavior*. Group membership is the proper basis for determining how any human being is to be treated. The Fascist says that loyal subjects will discriminate against all aliens. The Communist says that members of different economic classes are *ipso facto* enemies, regardless of their qualities as individuals.

We who have joined the movements to improve intergroup relations have rejected the dogmas of ideological barrier, immoral politics, and group prejudice. We have asserted three counter-propositions:

1. Persons of different nations and classes *can* avoid misunderstandings.

2. Everyone has moral obligations in his dealings with persons outside his own race and class.

3. Race prejudice and class prejudice are wrong.

These three repudiations of totalitarianism articulate the objectives to which I referred earlier when I said that there is not a full agreement on positive goals. If we were not preoccupied with the special menace of totalitarianism, I believe that we would all see that the ideal of good group relations requires more than the three injunctions: Avoid misunderstandings, avoid violence, and avoid group prejudice.

The survival of western civilization has required opposition to the outrageous purposes of the totalitarians. But the future course of civilization is not charted by negations. If you ask me where I am going, and I answer: "I refuse to go to Halifax," you will be justified in saying, "I am very glad to know that you are not going to Halifax, but will you kindly tell me exactly where you *are* going?"

It may be possible to show the false clarity of popular intergroup slogans by subjecting them to ethical analysis. By "ethical analysis" I mean not only the careful definition of the meaning of words but also an inquiry to discover whether the stated ideals are compatible with the mass of loyalties, interests, and convictions that have claims upon us.[6] Let us test the *scope* of our deliberations. When we assert the desirability of avoiding misunderstandings, violence, and prejudice, have we forgotten some incompatible values which claim our devotion at other times and places?

Take, for example, our rejection of the first totalitarian teaching about ideological barriers. We have faith in the processes of negotiation. We believe that men and women of different classes and races can communicate. But do we affirm the possibility of a complete meeting of minds on every subject? Do we assert that universal agreement on all matters is desirable? Grant that, up to a certain point, common understandings can be increased. Is it not possible that well-meaning talkers may open up a kind of Pandora's box by trying to go beyond the limits of human communication? May not human relations be worsened by trying to agree on too much?

I shall mention two relevant cases. When UNESCO arranged conferences on the subject of universal human rights, intellectuals from many cultures had surprisingly little trouble agreeing that every man has such rights as the right to a fair trial.[7] Then the intellectuals tried to agree on the ultimate reasons for such rights. They fell into controversy. Some of the delegates said that the rights were God-given. Others rejected any reference to theology. Some adhered to one philosophical system, some to another. They were at an impasse. As soon as they returned from ultimate justifications to specific actions and rights, they were once more in substantial agreement.

A similar limitation on intergroup harmonization has appeared in the National Conference of Christians and Jews. Jews, Catholics, and Protestants of many denominations have been able to agree on campaigns of public education, designed to reduce tensions. Yet, whenever interfaith programs of a religious nature were proposed, some of the constituents drew back. Anything resembling cooperative worship has provoked condemnation. As a result, the National Conference has limited its objectives. It undertakes to promote the cooperation of religiously motivated persons, but it avoids programs that require or might be thought to require agreement in theology, in liturgy, or in ecclesiastical loyalty.

Do these experiences in UNESCO and the National Conference cast doubt upon the goal of overcoming ideological barriers, improving communication, and securing agreements instead of going to war? They do suggest that people are not single-minded. Intergroup understanding is not the only goal. Most people are not expecting, for example, to overcome intergroup misunderstandings by abolishing group divisions. They not only look forward to the survival of their group; they value many of the folkways, the beliefs and sentiments, and the forms of organization which distinguish the groups to which they belong.

This is most apparent in the case of religious groups. Few of the men and women who are trying to control sectarian antagonisms would be willing to give up their own religion. They are against religious wars, but they also have their own religious loyalties. The same is obviously true with reference to nationality, and, to an undetermined extent, it is true of racial identity. In the United States, where successive waves of immigrants used to be greeted with the "melting pot" idea, it is no longer popular to define Americanization as the surrender of all ancestral customs and memories. If the immigrant learns the common language and shows respect for a few fundamental rights and duties, the rest of American culture is increasingly regarded, not as an amalgam, but as an orchestration, to use Kallen's happy word. Even ethnic groups that had lost their cultural roots have been reclaiming parts of their heritage. I refer to studies by Negro scholars, like Lorenzo Turner, identifying the African prototypes of the spirituals, the folk tales, and the vocabulary that Negroes can claim as their own contribution to the cultural wealth of America.[8]

On the international scene there has been a decline in "One-Worldism" of the kind which expected the early establishment of one universal language, one world government, one religion, one global economic system, and a single, all-comprehending educational system. Certain problems and enterprises are recognized as needing more than local regulation and quite possibly more than national regulation. Atomic energy is the outstanding case in point, and in western Europe the need for international government is seen with respect to the heavy industries, the currency system, and tariffs. But everywhere there is a jealous guarding of local autonomy in many of life's interests, and a hope that worldwide control of atomic energy, for example, will be compatible with local or regional independence in many other matters.

If we want both intergroup understanding and the preservation of group cultures, we are confronted by the problem of convincing the world that our group culture does not endanger the peace of the world. A ready-made theory exists for the peaceful coexistence of different religions. In this country and in other countries where Church and State have been separated, religion has been defined, not as public business but as a private affair. There are some exceptions to this rule—for example, when anyone refuses military service on religious grounds or when health regulations conflict with certain religious creeds. But, in general and for the most part, religious freedom and consequent religious variety seem tolerable. We may believe that the world would be much improved if our neighbor gave up his religion, but many of us agree with Jefferson that "whether my neighbor believes in no god or thirty gods neither robs my purse nor breaks my leg." Even if we disagree with Jefferson, we believe that any attempt on our part to use the power of the State to promote or suppress a creed would cause more harm than good.

If the distinction between public and private interest justifies the perpetuation of religious groupings, then the problem of avoiding intergroup misunderstandings takes on a new aspect. The problem now is to show that the preservation of this sect and that sect is not a threat to the public interest and the public peace. On this issue grave doubts are heard from time to time, especially with reference to the parochial schools. In dealing with these doubts, we are handicapped not only by a lack of information but also by a vagueness of theory concerning the public interest. There have been many studies of economic enterprise, and the public interest in economic matters is much better defined than formerly,[9] but surprisingly few studies have explored noneconomic groups to sharpen the definition of what is properly public and what is safely private.[10] Better theory on this point is badly needed.

The promotion of intergroup understanding, then, is an ambiguous and uncertain objective, if all we have in mind is to deny categorically the totalitarian dogmas about ideological barriers. No doubt, an exchange of some information about the beliefs and practices of various groups will reduce intergroup misunderstandings and remove the sources of irrational conflict. But since a universal amalgamation of all group cultures is not seriously contemplated, some fears of group idiosyncrasies may be rational and not all attempts to explain group differences will be successful. The problem is not only to mark off certain theological and philosophical areas as private sanctuaries, as has been done in UNESCO and in the National Conference, but also to develop the theory of the public interest so that a convincing defense can be offered for the compatibility of group creeds and rituals with the peace of the world.

I turn now to the second objective of intergroup friendship, viz., the rejection of the totalitarian belief in coercive force. Under twentieth-century conditions, the Fascist said, a ruling elite must use military force to bring order out of chaos. The Communists talk about the future withering away of the state, but right now they believe that the Communist Party must direct a dictatorship. Stalin reversed all tendencies to soften this doctrine by calling for increased coercion as a means of establishing the classless society in which coercion would be unnecessary.[11]

The intergroup education movement rejects the doctrine of the police state: that much is clear. But are good intergroup relations incompatible with any use of the police power? A reading of the current literature does not yield an unambiguous view of the police power. In fact, there are two opposed tendencies.

One tendency (among the group dynamics theorists) is to talk about the unwholesomeness of any power-enforced regime. Especially in the literature of industrial relations, there is a marshaling of evidence to show that coercion and discipline are often resorted to unnecessarily. It is asserted that uncooperative folk would voluntarily cooperate if given a little more time and a little better opportunity to understand the situation. There is much talk about the process of group discussion and its potentialities for producing unanimity. There are deprecations not only of physical violence and economic coercion but even of majority rule.[12] Obviously, this tendency to idealize persuasion and minimize the justifications for force leads us in the direction of anarchism. It is not a long jump from some of the group dynamics literature to Benjamin

Tucker, the Massachusetts anarchist, who decried majority rule because it meant the coercion of a minority. This line of thought reminds us of Emerson who, in his essay on "Politics," said that the State exists only to educate men and when it succeeds in educating men it removes the reason for its existence.

An opposing tendency is found in the demand of minority group representatives that the power of the State be used to secure and preserve their rights. The power of the federal government is enlisted to coerce local communities into desegregating the public schools. In many states legislation has been sought to permit legal action against those who do not follow fair employment practices. The assumption, often evident in these drives for antidiscriminatory legislation, is that society harbors an element that is not responsive to reason.[13]

One wing of the movement for better human relations inclines toward absolute faith in noncoercive measures. The other wing inclines toward the use of the police power of the State. This division does not reflect merely technical differences. It is not merely a division between those who understand the possibilities of group dynamics and those who do not. It is, I believe, a division between those whose attention is absorbed by the problems of peace and those whose attention is absorbed by the problems of justice. The values of peace and of justice are not easily reconciled.

This split suggests the need for broad studies of the conditions under which an appeal to force may be warranted. It may be that the group dynamics theorists, who put so much faith in persuasion, have concentrated their attention upon the small group process in which justice is more easily secured. The FEPC advocates, who lean toward legal coercion, may have focused on the larger community, where injustices are perpetuated by deadlocks and organizational breakdowns. Is there an ultimate difference between the potentialities of small groups and the larger public? This question can be raised without any presumption that Hegel was correct in contrasting the sentimentality appropriate to the family and the Machiavellian politics appropriate to the State.[14] It is quite possible that idealism can succeed at the high levels of public business, but that such public idealism may require techniques that are different in kind from those that work in the small group.

What would be the design of an investigation that might give us a clear and positive goal instead of a mere revulsion against the police state? In casting about for a suggestion I have wondered whether Thomas Hill Green, the English idealist, did not have a fruitful idea. Green thought that governmental institutions are not moral in any ordinary sense that would imply the absence of coercion, but he said that governments should create the *conditions* under which citizens may live moral lives without a resort to force.[15] Political and legal measures, he believed, should set up "hindrances to hindrances"; they could correct conditions that interfere with moral behavior.

Following Green's thought we can imagine several types of situation. In Nazi Germany we had the horrible example of a State itself setting up hindrances to moral action. Gentiles were prohibited by law from behaving decently toward the Jews. A similar misuse of state power is seen in South Africa and in some local American jurisdictions where law makes it impossible for a white man to deal fairly with a Negro.

A second type of situation is one in which the State says nothing about the treatment of Jews or Negroes or any other group. There is legal freedom, which does not guarantee moral behavior, but at the same time moral behavior is permitted.

A third type of situation would exist where the State may be silent on intergroup relations, but there is an extra-legal force in the community that has the same effect as a segregation law. We recall the Ku Klux Klan, the gentlemen's agreements and restrictive covenants, sometimes enforced by terrorism. These extra-legal practices may reflect the general state of public opinion, but often they represent the intimidating activity of a minority, coercing the majority by arousing fears of retaliation or of unfair competition. In the second instance, there would seem to be a need for positive State action against the intimidating minority. By using the force of law the State might assure ordinary citizens an opportunity to follow their conscience.

I have tried to describe conditions that would warrant such measures as FEPC and desegregation orders. My purpose has not been to settle the issue of such legislation in New York or Georgia or South Africa but rather to indicate the kind of evidence that would be relevant. By some such study the ideal of less violent human relations could be transformed from a mere rejection of totalitarianism into a constructive affirmation.

A broader theoretical foundation is also needed for the third intergroup ideal, viz., the ideal of nondiscrimination. We are said to have obligations to respect the rights of persons outside our own group and we are told that discrimination on account of race, nationality, or religion is wrong. This is a disapproval of the Fascist ideal of preferential treatment for their own nationals. It is also a rejection of the Communist ideal of friendliness within one's own class and hostility toward all other classes.

Again, I believe, it is not sufficient to stop with a negation. The incompleteness of the ideal of nondiscrimination is apparent as soon as we ask, Avoid discrimination on account of skin color for what purpose? A man does not satisfy a high moral standard by saying, "I don't discriminate: I hate everyone." Neither can a man be praised for saying: "I don't discriminate. I will vote for anyone. I am willing to give scholarships to anyone. I will do business with anyone."

Are we not urged to avoid ancestral discrimination in order that we may discriminate on the basis of individual merit? Although drives against discrimination sometimes sound as if every man is to be king, we usually retreat to the position that opportunities should be equalized. Mental giants are to have a chance to perform great tasks, regardless of ancestry. Pygmies and ne'er-do-wells are to receive modest rewards, regardless of ancestry. I believe that the purpose of nondiscrimination on the basis of race and religion is to establish a community in which men may discriminate according to competence and common interest. It can hardly be seriously proposed that everyone must associate with everyone else. Intellectuals and lowbrows, for example, bore one another. Athletes and persons of sedentary disposition do not usually seek each other's company. A good society is not one in which everyone must bore and irritate everyone else. A good society is rather one in which citizens have the right of free association and contact, within the limits of public policy.

A taboo on discrimination, therefore, is attractive because we believe in discriminating on the basis of actual ability and interest. And why select men according to their ability? Because of an economic interest in getting the important work of the world done and getting it done with some efficiency.

This economic goal does not always call for a simple taboo on group discriminations. It may, when the enterprise is sectarian, require selection within the sectarian group. The relevance of ancestral grouping in determining competence is, perhaps, apparent in deciding who is ready and able to perform religious duties and tasks. A sectarian college, for example, may lose its usefulness in preparing leaders for its sect if it does not give preference to children who are born into families belonging to the sect. Fitness for living up to marriage vows also seems to be affected by sectarian origins. Furthermore, there is the problem of loyalties in the appointment of persons who belong to sects that deny the legitimacy of secular loyalties. The ideal of "no religious discrimination" has complications that are not present in the ideal of "no racial discrimination."

There is another difficulty in the objective of nondiscrimination. If equality of opportunity is the only rule, then the slow-witted, those lacking in social grace, the cripples, are doomed to a sad existence, regardless of race, nationality, or creed. This goes counter to humanitarianism which, in former times, called for charity, and in our day calls for minimum living standards throughout the community. It is only necessary to mention this humanitarianism in order to show that some line must be drawn between guaranteed rights, on the one hand, and privileges that have to be earned, on the other hand. Every person is entitled to police and fire protection, regardless of personal merit. Every person, however incompetent, is entitled to a minimum of medical care. Every child is entitled to protection against starvation and ignorance. In many jurisdictions it has been decided that every aged person, regardless of the worth of his past contributions to society, is entitled to minimum old age benefits.

Where do we draw the line? In order to draw a line between benefits that shall be freely available without any discrimination and rewards that shall be given by discrimination of personal merit, we need additional light from the experience of economists, medical men, social workers, lawyers, and others who have been dealing with indigence and the distribution of income. We need to know what society can afford.

In one sentence, what I have been trying to say is this: our ideals of improved human relations require better use of certain social sciences and practical arts that, thus far, have not been in the forefront of the intergroup education movements.[16] Sociologists, psychologists, and educators have rendered signal service by filling gaps in our knowledge about language and attitude. They have showed how we may hope to live in the twentieth century without resorting to totalitarianism. They have debunked the totalitarian justifications of group prejudice and the totalitarian theories about the impossibility of intergroup communication. But the full development of the arts of intergroup relations requires a broader theoretical foundation than the analysis of prejudice and the technique of discussion.

Research into the improvement of communication needs to identify the feasible and essential areas of communication and agreement. Research into the improvement of voluntary cooperation needs a sharper definition of the circumstances under which legal coercion is justified. Research on the subjects of prejudice and discrimination needs a better understanding of the benefits that can be universally available and the benefits for which only equality of opportunity can be guaranteed.

Total agreement is not an intelligent alternative to total war. Blind passivity is not an intelligent alternative to fanatical aggression. An absence of judgment is not an intelligent alternative to irrational prejudgment. The intelligent alternatives to totalitarianism will be based on more than the ability to say "No" to the new barbarians. We want to avoid misunderstandings, but we also want to preserve group values. We want to reduce violence, but we also want justice. We want to avoid irrational prejudice, but we also want work well done. We want friendship among human groups, but not peace at any price. We want peace with public safety, with justice, and with a reasonable degree of efficiency.

FOOTNOTES TO CHAPTER I

1. See Robin M. Williams, Jr., *The Reduction of Intergroup Tensions*, Social Science Research Council, New York, 1947; Alfred J. Marrow, *Living Without Hate*, pp. x, 1, Harper and Brothers, New York, 1951; Dorwin Cartwright and Alvin Zander, *Group Dynamics*, pp. ix, 5, Row, Peterson & Company, Evanston, Ill., 1953; Muzafer Sherif and Carolyn W. Sherif, *Groups in Harmony and Tension*, p. 1, Harper and Brothers, New York, 1953; *Annual Review of Psychology*, *1955*, p. 212, Stanford University Press, Stanford, Calif., 1955; Marie Jahoda, *Studies in the Scope and Method of "The Authoritarian Personality,"* p. 12, Free Press, Glencoe, Ill., 1954; L. and E. Cook, *Intergroup Education*, p. 3, McGraw-Hill Book Co., New York, 1954.

2. Carl Schmitt, *Der Begriff des Politischen*, 1927.

3. Alfred Rosenberg, *Der Mythus des XX Jahrhundert*, 1930.

4. Ludwig Müller, *Deutsche Gotteswort*, 1936, trans. into English under the title, *The Germanization of the New Testament*, Friends of Europe Publication no. 64, London. Excerpts are accessible to American readers in Chandler's *Rosenberg's Nazi Myth*, p. 111, Cornell University Press, Ithaca, N.Y., 1945.

5. V. I. Lenin, *What Is To Be Done?*, 1902.

6. I have discussed the nature of moral deliberation and its improvement by ethical analysis in *Ethics for Policy Decisions*, Prentice-Hall, New York, 1952. Because of the complexities of our loyalties, etc., there seems to be no single test by which we may make sure that a prima-facie obligation is "really" a duty. The practical problem of appraising our first impressions and impulses appears to require an exploration of the compatibility of any proposed ideal with many convictions. The difficulty exists, whether one believes that all moral notions are ultimately derived from one authoritative source or whether one accepts an emotivist theory and says that things are right just because some individual or some group feels that way.

7. See UNESCO, *Human Rights*, Columbia University Press, New York, 1949. See also W. K. Frankena, "The Concept of Universal Human Rights," in *Science, Language, and Human Rights*, pp. 189ff, University of Pennsylvania Press, Philadelphia, 1952. For the comments of one member of the Committee of Experts, see Richard McKeon, "Philosophic Differences and the Issues of Freedom," *Ethics* LXI. 106, Jan. 1951.

8. See Lorenzo D. Turner, *Africanisms in the Gullah Dialect*, University of Chicago Press, Chicago, 1949. Since the publication of this book Professor Turner has collected many materials in west Africa to support even stronger claims concerning the survival of African culture traits in the United States. The psychological need for membership in groups that are smaller than "mankind in general" has been described by psychiatrists, and in this paper I shall assume that the desire to "belong" is a legitimate desire.

9. Even Socialists have admitted that complete public control of economic enterprise is unnecessary. See Sir Oliver Franks, *Central Planning and Control in War and Peace*, Harvard University Press, Cambridge, Mass., 1947. A simple illustration of the subtler delineations of the public domain is traffic regulation. The public interest is asserted in the stoplights and in regulations governing the manner of driving, but it is usually thought unnecessary to dictate the motorists'

destinations. In other words, we are getting away from the all-or-none positions which characterized nineteenth-century debates between Socialists and laissez-faire economists.

10. See Herbert W. Schneider, "Political Morality," in *American Philosophy Today and Tomorrow*, ed. by Kallen and Hook, pp. 435f, Lee Furman, New York, 1935.

11. J. Stalin, *Report to the Seventeenth Congress* of the Communist Party of the Soviet Union, 1934.

12. See, for example, the comment of N. Maier, "Improving Supervision through Training," in *The Psychology of Labor-Management Relations*, p. 27, Industrial Relations Research Association, Champaign, Ill., 1949.

13. According to one rather common misreading of Adorno's *The Authoritarian Personality*, a fraction of mankind is hopelessly and inevitably Fascist.

14. F. Hegel, *The Philosophy of Right*, 1821; Dyde translation, 1896.

15. Thomas Hill Green, *Lectures on the Principles of Political Obligation*, Longmans, Green, New York, 1891.

16. See the UNESCO volume, *Humanism and Education in East and West*, 1953, and the UNESCO document for the 1954 Indian Philosophical Congress Symposium on "Human Rights and International Obligations."

CHAPTER II

The American Catholic

JOHN LAFARGE, S.J.

Our purpose in discussing American Catholicism is to describe, not to offer any ultimate appraisal. What evaluation we offer is merely relative—the relevance of a certain specific religious movement to the general pattern of American life and American problems. Yet even a description can be too baldly descriptive to achieve its own purpose. One can construct a tremendous picture of American Catholicism; yet the facts are difficult to understand unless we take into account the inner impetus that has generated the facts. Otherwise we assemble a disjointed collection of data. Outwardly they seem related, but inwardly they lack cohesion.

In my childhood I used to be delighted with old picture books that Commodore Matthew Galbraith Perry, of Japanese fame, brought home with him from his expedition to that country. Japanese artists had meticulously depicted every detail of the American fleet. From sailors' descriptions they portrayed the mechanical wonders of the United States, such as railroads, down to such small details as pistons, cogs, and safety valves, but none of the details hooked together. The pistons did not turn the wheels, the wheels were not connected with any drive shaft, and the locomotives carried groups of ladies drinking tea as they perched on the boilers. It was an assemblage of exact details with no real coherence. Rube Goldberg would be infinitely more intelligible than these highly decorative offerings prepared for the delight of the inquisitive Japanese populace.

So, too, we could describe a great religious phenomenon with apparently the utmost factual accuracy, yet be as far from reality as were the Tokyo artist's locomotives, simply because we missed the idea which makes the whole assemblage operate.

The immense complex of United States Catholicism, with all its activities and outward manifestations, springs from one central vision. In this vision there are elements common to both Judaism and Protestantism. There are also elements which are specific to Catholicism. I do not attempt to distinguish them in my brief description. But I find when I speak of Catholicism that those of other faiths are apt to say: "Why, this is ours as well."

Briefly stated, Catholicism is a vision of salvation and liberation, an *ultimate* liberation and salvation, imperishable heritage of the eternal possession of God. Also there is a vision of *proximate* liberation and salvation. In a negative sense it means liberation from the roots of evil, whether the personal evil of our own deeds or the cosmic evil which perverts and corrupts the human being. And in a positive sense it means a life into which we are initiated in the waters of baptism, with their accompanying pledge of an ultimate share in the glory of Christ's Resurrection.

This liberation and salvation are accessible to all mankind throughout the world, without exception of race, color, or condition, through association with a Divine Redeemer. This association is achieved through faith and love on the part of man and a special grace of light and strength given by the Creator. Grace comes to man in a sacramental fashion, through his incorporation into a religious community; and this community carries the message and the person of the Redeemer to all times and places. The Redeemer's teachings, and His sacramental presence, imply a correlative response of faith, of worship, and of personal commitment.

The outward expression of this vision meets, however, with a special difficulty; the outward armature of language and form meets the eye, rather than the interior vision. The life of the Church, as a visible society, is conditioned, like the life of man, by the physical elements of time and space. There is a special difficulty for the Catholic to transcend this outward armature since so much of the communication is apt to be couched in traditional language. Even the use of sacramental symbols is conditioned by the imaginative context of the social community in which the sacramental action operates. Breaking bread and anointing with oils do not carry the vivid connotations of fraternity or of royal or priestly dignity that they had in the ancient world. Their meaning has to be interpreted. Religion, therefore, as a response to this inner vision meets with certain *obstacles*. The obstacles themselves are a sociologically significant phenomenon. At the same time they manifest certain *trends* which the Catholic Faith by its own inner dynamism strives to overcome.

I

Obstacles and trends may conveniently be conceived as related to several major categories by which this religious movement takes concrete form—for instance, as a minority, or as an institution, or a culture, or as an active spiritual life. Let us consider these separately.

Historically American Catholicism is a minority not only numerically but also in the sense that it came to this country when its political framework, the main social structure and mores, were clearly determined by Protestantism. As Richard Niebuhr observes in *The Kingdom of God in America*, the United States was a land in which Protestantism had its first chance to build a culture. Hence this Catholic minority had to undertake a prodigious problem of adaptation and assimilation once the great tide of immigration had set in. Works like *The Life of James Cardinal Gibbons*, by John Tracy Ellis, Catholic University of America; *The Life of Archbishop Carroll*, by Peter Guilday; and *The German Catholics in America*, by Coleman Barry, O.S.B., initiate us into the great controversies which enlivened this earlier period of assimilation,

controversies in which Rochester's famous Bishop Bernard Mc-
Quaid played so prominent a part.

I do not attempt to summarize the past. In our brief time it
is merely possible to glance at certain phenomena of the present.
One of the most striking aspects of Catholicism as it is today in
the United States is the extent to which it is at home, as it were, in
the United States. It is true that among the Catholics, numbering
thirty million souls, there are still certain elements of division based
upon various national origins and linguistic differences, but with
each newer generation these become rapidly minimized, as Will
Herberg subtly notes in his recent book, *Protestants, Catholics, and
Jews*. Affiliation to one or another of the three great prevailing
religious divisions of the United States, or rather religious categories, has become in a curious way a mark of public identification
with America. To be identified with a religious body is in a way
a condition of being identified with our country itself, a phenomenon which undoubtedly is partly the effect of the experiences of
the Second World War. When people ask now what you "are,"
you no longer say "I am an Irishman" (or a German, or an old-
line American); you simply say "I am a Baptist" (or a Catholic, or
a Jew). Whether I work much or little at my particular faith, it
gives me a sort of being in the community; so much so, that if a
man aspires to be President of the United States and has not been
working so hard at his religion, he must take steps immediately to
"be" something or other of an ecclesiastical nature. Hence this
phenomenon, as Mr. Herberg observes, has brought Catholicism
squarely in line with the great American way. Such a popular
identification could create no end of confusion if understood as
meaning that any person is a good American simply because he
or she is affiliated with some religious body. Religion teaches certain fundamental virtues which every good American should possess. But to be a good American, in the full sense of the term, one
needs, at the very least, to know something of the history of our
country and of its Constitution, and their relation to the great civic
issues of our time. And these are matters which religion, as such,
does not undertake to teach. But if you mean that to be *a religious
person* is one of the normal and, indeed, necessary marks of a gen-
uine American, and conversely that an irreligious or antireligious

spirit is contrary to American tradition and principles, then one
might agree to this (obviously superficial and simply extrinsic)
identification.

The institutional life of the Church, of which material structures
are a manifestation, is affected by the context in which it operates.
It cannot help taking somewhat of the shape of the secular world.
No matter how idealistic the aims of a church-related school, it
has to conform for its very existence to the standards of accrediting
agencies and prevailing modes in athletics, college usages, etc. In
raising money it must follow a fixed and standardized pattern laid
down by the usages of the community. Hence there is a certain
duality in Catholic thought on this matter of our educational institutions. On the one hand, there is a widespread prevailing
gratitude, a legitimate pride in the achievement. No country in
the world has built so tremendous an independent educational
structure, inspired by the highest religious ideals, as has the Catholic Church in America. Catholics traveling abroad find it very
difficult to explain even to their highly educated foreign brethren
the real scope, variety, and competence of Catholic America's
schools, ranging from the kindergarten and primary school straight
through to the college, the graduate school, to the highest reaches
of humanistic and technical and theological education. We look
back in gratitude now to the great pioneers, who stanchly held for
the principles of religious schools. We are proud and grateful for
the thousands of splendid men and women who have consecrated
themselves, often under the greatest privation, to developing and
staffing this system of education. On the other hand, many an
anxious thought is given to the vexing demands of the present moment: the ever-increasing financial burden, the exacting requirements of specialization, and the problems of overcrowding and a
scarcity of teachers which we share with all other institutions in
this country. What changes may be made in Church policy in this
matter are a matter of conjecture which I do not enter into, since
my purpose is merely to show the sociological phenomenon, not
to engage in prophecy.

In contrast to a certain type of educational monism which is
represented by a small but vociferous and articulate minority in the
United States, Catholic educational theory holds vigorously to the

doctrine of educational pluralism. We have no desire to impose our own schools on others. We are, moreover, most anxious to cooperate in every way with non-Catholic or secular schools in every means and fashion by which culture can be advanced. The Catholic separate school is emphatically not a separatist school; and even if individuals may at times have talked in separatist tones, it is not the spirit of Catholic education. On the contrary, every manner of cooperation between the Catholic Church-related school and the schools of other denominations or no denomination is essential to the welfare of the community, and I think it is clearly recognized as such by leading Catholic educators. We do not find any sanction either in natural justice or in the Constitution of the United States for the notion that the tax-supported state school is the one and only model of American education, or that its products are in any way necessarily closer to the core of Americanism than those trained in the church-related or private school. Indeed, the problem is constantly becoming more actual. Educators are becoming more and more convinced that not only the home and church, but the school itself must make its contribution to the desperately needed spiritual strengthening of our youth. Yet the very intensity of this need emphasizes the difficulty of making such a spiritual contribution through our public schools as they are constituted—hence the importance of a pluralist educational philosophy as at least a partial solution to an evident dilemma. It is this larger view, this pluralist view, this cooperative view which is gaining in strength, in my estimation, among people of various beliefs at the present time.

On the other hand, American Catholicism does not urge the full implications of state recognition of religious schools. It is perfectly reconciled to bearing its own burden cheerfully and consistently, hard as this burden is. It prefers to carry its own burden rather than to lose its spirit of educational independence and is content to demand only those auxiliary services such as health services, public transportation, and, in some states, free textbooks, which are the allotment not to the school as such or to any particular form of education but to the personal needs of the individual child as a citizen of the state. The educational program takes its meaning from a spiritual ideal, a spiritual vision. Here again we need to look more closely at the great underlying concept; here, too, I think it important to note the idea of the Church itself. Alien to Catholic thought is the idea of progressively realizing the Church itself as an increasingly perfect entity. On the contrary, the Catholic conceives the Church as a perfect institution, in itself unchanging and adapted to the end to which its Divine Founder destined it. But men's realization of the Church, her principles, her teaching, her practice, is contingent on human wills and on the fickleness of history. So it is that while the ultimate spiritual ideal of the Church remains unchanged, each and every age and country has its own trends toward realizing this ideal and correspondingly particular phases that appeal to the peoples of a certain place and epoch.

II

In the United States today we may notice two great trends among American Catholics. One is the movement inward toward the inner life; the other is the outgoing movement, a sense of mission to the entire world.

The movement toward the inner life increases in variety and extent with every year. One of its most striking manifestations is that of the movement for closed retreats: periods of from two or three to six or eight days spent in solitude, meditation, and careful planning, retreats practiced by men and women in every walk of life from teen-agers on. Again there is the startling growth of contemplation, as seen in the vocations to contemplative religious Orders. A short drive from the University of Rochester is the recent Trappist foundation at Piffard, New York. Practically the entire community, including the newly elected Abbot himself, I have heard are young men. I was asked the other day how to explain this development of the contemplative life, this growth of inwardness. You can venture many explanations if you like, but the simplest one is that given me this summer by President Pusey of Harvard, speaking of certain developments in his own organization: "Why not just call it the grace of God?" Again we are recording simply the facts and not speculating as to the origins, but we find continually increasing demand for books dealing with the inner life, with the great problems of existence, of suffering, of

destiny, of ultimate hope.   And this is all the more striking because
this tendency seems to increase with the increase of a generalized
prosperity in the United States.   I am not referring to the so-called
religious boom, the seeking for various kinds of peace-of-mind and
peace-of-soul recipes about which so much is said and written.
This is a deeper, much less self-centered movement, a seeking to
face reality in all its harsh nakedness rather than to escape from it.

III

Turning from the inward trends we note in American Catholicism a greater participation with regard to the problems of the
nation.   Two World Wars have brought with them a tremendous
contribution of Catholic personnel to the defense of the nation,
along with the contributions of the other great religious groups.
At the same time there has been a corresponding growth of
thought, of interest, and of action in trying to find a specifically
religious solution for our common American problems.   American
Catholics, considered as a large social group, are no longer deeply
concerned about mere survival, about establishing a foothold in
the New World.   It is less today a question of preserving, in hostile
surroundings, a certain pattern of life inherited from the social
structure of the Catholic homeland.   Rather they seek to reach
the minds and hearts of the general community, help to vindicate
certain spiritual elements of moral integrity, and so help to establish a pattern of social life in the United States in which Catholics
and non-Catholics alike may live, move, and have their moral being.

For the Catholic mind, integrity in domestic issues, the integrity
of the home and the family, is traditionally of paramount concern,
a concern of both sexes.   In the words of Pope Pius XII, speaking
to the women of Italy on August 15, 1945:

> The fate of the family, the fate of human relations are at stake.
> They are in your hands.   Every woman has . . . the strict obliga-
> tion in conscience, not to absent herself, but to go into action in a
> manner and way suitable to the condition of each so as to hold back
> those currents which threaten the home, so as to oppose those doc-
> trines which undermine its foundations, so as to prepare, organize
> and achieve its restoration. . . . Both [man and woman] have the

right and duty to cooperate toward the total good of society and of
their country. . . .

Let us take the case of civil rights: These are at present the same
for both, but with how much more discernment and efficacy will
they be utilized if man and woman come to complement one another. . . . The sensitiveness and fine feeling proper to woman . . .
are . . . of immense help when it is a question of throwing light on
the needs, aspirations and dangers that touch domestic, public welfare or religious spheres.

In recent times the Catholic Family movement, centered in
Washington, D.C., has attained a surprising popularity, as has a
similar undertaking, the Cana Conferences, centered in St. Louis,
Missouri. In both instances, the attack upon the family problem
is on a positive basis; reconstruction of the family as an integrated
unit of society through the cooperation and intensive participation of married people, particularly young married couples. They
are themselves moved to concern for social action, a paramount
question for religious people all over the world. The social action
movement of American Catholicism is a direct heir of the various
European Catholic Social Action movements, which in their origin
date back to the beginnings of the industrial revolution a little
over a hundred years ago, but were more formally inaugurated
with the famous encyclical *Rerum Novarum* (On the Condition of
the Workingman) issued by Pope Leo XIII in 1891. In 1931
his successor twice removed, Pope Pius XI, complained in another
encyclical, *Quadragesimo Anno* (On the Reconstruction of the
Social Order) that the lessons of Leo had been taken to heart only
very partially, especially by the employing groups. The advent
of Communism brought the matter to particular urgency and more
and more anxiety grew concerning the profound separation between the industrial proletariat and the Church, a phenomenon
which is most extreme in France and was highly dramatized there
by the enterprise of the Priest Workers. In the Latin countries
this division between the employer and the working classes, particularly the working proletariat, still remains a number one problem. The suspicion and often strongly anticlerical spirit of the
workers encountered traditional rigidity and extreme economic
conservatism on the side of the employers. This resulted in a basic
lack of communication between the two groups.

In the United States this situation, as we know, is considerably different. Whatever our social economic problems may be here, the American worker is not characterized by the extreme class consciousness of the European. Furthermore, the employing element in our United States economy believes in a philosophy of production and widespread consumption which he often combines with a very distinct idealism.

Hence, the social action programs of American Catholics, both clergy and lay, have been centered very largely on creating a greater sense of responsibility and intelligent leadership among the labor groups and combating a materialistic, self-aggrandizing spirit, as well as in trying to inculcate a sense of social responsibility in management itself.

While the social action work of the Catholic Church in the United States is officially centered in the Social Action Department of the National Catholic Welfare Conference in Washington, nevertheless much of it is in the form of private or local initiative, in which the Social Action Department acts more as a clearing house, a general service station for the work around the country, than as an actual directing influence. Variety of concepts, techniques, and approaches is not only understood but is positively encouraged. Characteristically American is the development of social-action work in the foreign missions attended by American Catholic personnel. In many of these, because of the depressed and primitive character of the populations with whom the missionaries operate, the more dynamic features of economic social action are more readily developed; examples are the cooperative movement in the American Jesuit missions of Jamaica in the West Indies, or British Honduras, or in India, the Maryknoll missionaries in South America and elsewhere, and the Franciscan missions among the American Indians of the Southwest. The Social Action movement is gaining the earnest enthusiastic attention of many of our Catholic university and college groups.

IV

Foreign observers to this country have frequently noticed that the major division in the United States is not so much that of

economic classes as across the racial lines. It is there that the most
painful lack of communication is evident. Hence comes the preoccupation of the Church with the question of race relations.

The interracial question in the past is much too complicated to
be treated in this very brief discourse. Its different phases, dating
from the period before the Civil War until the present, have been
accurately summed up in the September, 1954, issue of *Jubilee*
magazine.*

In its earlier, more traditional form the problem of racial minorities, such as that of the largest racial minority in the United States,
the Negro, was considered more from the standpoint of beneficent
work for a given racial milieu. As such it was mission work, in the
larger sense of the term. This intraracial work covers a great
variety of undertakings providing for the various needs of a social
group and affording them equal or even special pastoral ministra-
tions.

In some of its forms such work was and today still is, though in
ever-lessening degree, conducted on a segregated basis. This phase,
conceived originally from a constructive and benevolent point of
view, became an obstacle and, indeed, a scandal in later years. The
Church's schools, societies, and various types of social welfare
work form part of the picture, varying in degrees of scope and
method.

But in its later phase, developed during the last twenty years, a
far-seeing element among American Catholics of both races has
become much more concerned with the racial situation itself.
Many of those who were devoted to intraracial work found that
they came up against positive roadblocks in their own special
undertakings because of the barrier of racial discrimination.
Movements of discontent and protest, crystallizing discriminatory
patterns either in general society or in the Church itself, became
channeled into a new form of active, fruitful cooperation, especially on an educational basis.

The official position of American Catholicism has become greatly
clarified of late and there is no further question thereon. The
racial issue in itself is fairly simple, not troubled by the technical

* This magazine may be secured from the publishers, at 377 Fourth Avenue,
New York, N.Y.

intricacies of the ethics of economic production, marketing, and distribution. The question rather is that of applying these fairly simple ideas to the vast complex texture of American life and thought, to realizing them under the most diverse circumstances. In other words, it is more or less the problem faced by every extensive work in public relations.

By the time of the Supreme Court decision of May 17, 1954, outlawing racial segregation in the nation's tax-supported schools, Catholic authorities were found to be already prepared for the situation. Several of the Church authorities in the very states where the segregational pattern obtained either legally or as a matter of entrenched custom had taken a bold stand for integration in their schools. Others soon followed suit. In twelve different states of the same complexion, various degrees of integration were already introduced or were already on their way. The firm stand of Archbishop Ritter of St. Louis, of Archbishop O'Boyle of Washington, of Bishop Vincent S. Waters of Raleigh, North Carolina, and Archbishop Rummel of New Orleans obtained nationwide prominence. What particularly attracted attention in many cases was the interesting fact that the authority of the Church, which arouses so many misgivings in the public mind, in each and every one of these cases turned out to be a strong safeguard of civil liberties and of religious integrity. This was most dramatically illustrated when, on October 7, 1955, the authority of the Archbishop of New Orleans was exercised to rebuke the conduct of certain white laymen who had refused to a Catholic Negro priest opportunity to officiate in one of the churches of the New Orleans Archdiocese. The Archbishop's attitude met with instant and public commendation from Rome. In the words of Archbishop Rummel:

It is the teaching of Holy Mother Church that every human being, regardless of race, color or nationality, is created after the image and likeness of God. . . . Thus every human being, regardless of race, color or nationality, is entitled to individual respect and consideration; even when by his conduct he proves himself unworthy, he is entitled to the definite considerations of justice and charity in conformity with the principles for which Christ died upon the cross for all men.

Let it be noted, to avoid any possible misunderstandings, that the interracial work of the Catholic Church in the United States is not organized as such on a national basis, like many other forms of Catholic activities. It is left to the initiative of individual dioceses or individual localities, but the result is a surprising unanimity of attitude and conduct. The twenty-five Catholic Interracial Councils of the United States, each of them organized separately and under the respective Church authority of the locality, are served and stimulated by the central office of the Catholic Interracial Council of New York at 20 Vesey Street.

As a result of this activity, the past twenty years have seen an astonishing transformation of Catholic attitude in schools, churches, institutions of every variety, and national and local organizations, as well as in the personal attitude of individuals. Particularly notable both as an effect and as a contributing cause has been the transformation in the Catholic press, which reaches many millions of readers every week. From one end of the country to the other the Catholic press has taken up the interracial cause, and in so doing they have been seconded by a surprising degree of friendliness and cooperation with Catholic effort on the part of the very influential and extensive weekly Negro press of the United States.

Mention of racial minorities points the way to the world situation. Experience in this country, especially within the last twelve months or so, has initiated us to the idea, so foreign to us formerly, that those whom we look upon as the least significant part of our population link us in point of fact with the majority populations of the world.

V

As members of the world Church, American Catholics enjoy an increasing sense of the world community, a sense of what Catholicity *as* Catholicity signifies. One phase of this development is a growing consciousness of the international community of Catholics and the corresponding obligation of the races.

The Second World War introduced Catholic youth of the United States to mission congregations in far-off Asia and Africa, as well as to the life of the Catholic Church in the old nations of Europe. Large sectors of American Catholics have relatives in countries behind the Iron Curtain and every phase of the "cold war" is of intimate concern to hundreds of thousands of Catholic families in the United States. In this way the picture of a world Church evolves in the mind of American Catholics from being merely a notional picture, something you have learned in an abstract fashion in the catechism, into a vision of a spiritual world community. There is a growing sense, too, of what a world Church like our own can do for all men, the vast realm of opportunity that it opens up for cooperation with people of every circumstance, of every belief.

One of the most striking instances of this development has been the evolution of the National Catholic Rural Life Conference, which began some thirty years ago as a means of reaching and encouraging scattered farm populations in this country and assisting them with religious information and better pastoral care, and at the same time encouraging Catholics to retain their roots in the land. Associated from the beginning with the work of the Catholic Rural Life Conference was cooperation with the older, more experienced secular or non-Catholic organizations in this field, such as the American Country Life Association. In recent years, thanks in large measure to the dynamic personality of its Executive Secretary, Monsignor Luigi Ligutti, the Rural Life Conference has stepped out onto the great stage of international work. It is cooperating as a consultant with the international agencies, such as the Food and Agriculture Association, the World Health Organization, and with the various forms of technical assistance provided either by the United Nations or by the United States. American Catholicism has found a new scope for its activities in the work of resettlement. Characteristic of this trend is the plan recently matured for the resettlement of seventy-five hand-picked Italian families in the state of South Carolina. Intended as a model pilot project for resettlement under religious auspices in one of the southern states, it is a work in which my own Archbishop, Francis Cardinal Spellman, is deeply interested.

VI

It would be easy to prolong these desultory remarks, but I would crowd your patience if I were to elaborate further the scope and opportunities of the world community. Let me conclude this very scanty and inadequate survey by mentioning another trend, less understood, much more tentative, but yet intensely significant and important at the present moment: the work of American Catholicism in the problems of the local community.

The local community is becoming the front line for ethnic and social divisions in the United States. It is there within the next few years that our major battles will have to be fought with poverty, ignorance, prejudice, discrimination, and all the host of social evils.

The theory of Catholic participation in civic community activities has not as yet been fully developed. There is still considerable discussion as to how far it should rest upon a parish basis, from the institutional aspect of the Church, or on a basis of the larger, the inter-parish unit or the diocese itself. One thing, however, is certain: that American Catholics are coming to appreciate the importance and value of active cooperation by their own Church, both as a moral force and as an institution, with the other moral forces and institutions in the community, to sense the need to unite all forces for decency and righteousness, in order to make a better America not just on some grandiose scale but right in our own neighborhoods. Experience in this line has been extremely fruitful, and I believe that Catholic thought has produced a number of new and original contributions, such as those worked out by some of our Catholic interracial councils and other community groups, in Chicago, Brooklyn, and Philadelphia.

American Catholicism is going through a period of development and transition. Just what ultimate forms it will take it would be useless to prophesy, for they will undoubtedly be determined in many ways through the course of history itself. But of one thing we can be certain: that the sense of contribution, its need and its possibilities, is bound to grow among American Catholics and at the same time the realization of its possibility will grow among all

those who are not of our faith.   We in this country are writing a
frontier epic, writing it in countless neighborhoods of the United
States.   This epic is a product of the mobile age in which we live;
it grows out of the clash and interplay of the social forces which
meet in our growing communities.   Like the old frontier of a
century or more ago, the new frontier is determining the kind of
country that we and our children shall live in.   It is a battleground
for conflicting interests; but it is also a theater for the highest kind
of disinterested justice and love.   Most specially, it is a field where
the nation's religious forces are playing a leading role.   The difficulties it involves should not blind us to the steady progress that is
being made, to the real triumphs that are being achieved.

If this is true of the local community, how much truer it is of the
vast international community!   According to Pope Pius XII:

> Catholics are saddled with a great responsibility. They above all,
> that is to say, must realize that they are called upon to overcome
> every vestige of nationalistic narrowness, and to seek a genuine fra-
> ternal encounter of nation with nation.[1]

How far Catholics, or American Catholics, or people of any
sort are living up to such responsibility, rests upon the decisions
each person takes in the depths of his own heart.   This is beyond
the scope of our brief survey.   But it will encourage us if we think
we discern a trend in this direction.

FOOTNOTE   TO   CHAPTER   II

1. Discourse, December 6, 1953, in *The Catholic Mind*, America Press, New
York, 1954.

CHAPTER III

The United States Indian

JOHN COLLIER

I believe that this Institute on Minority Groups, and the research enterprises on this varied topic, here at the University of Rochester, are significant and truly important. My one generalized remark has to do with the discussion program of the Institute. The prevailing, professed or unprofessed, popular view in America assumes that ethnic and cultural minorities are perishing quantities, soon to become devoured by, assimilated into, the universe of other-directed life. (The phrase and concept "other-directed" are lifted from that brilliant, withal limited, work of David Riesman, *The Lonely Crowd*.) I am glad to see that "The American Catholic" is the preceding topic and "The American Jew" the one that follows. Anyone, or almost anyone, will recognize that the Catholic and the Jew, in the United States and the world, are not perishing quantities, and are not losing their souls in the process of gaining the world. There—in the Catholic and the Jew—are living histories going back to the roots of things, keeping their genius, delivering it into the world, and thereby intensifying also their own cultural and individual genius, which is not going to die.

And this way it is and will be with the American Indian, most evidently in the Hemisphere—in the Andes, in Middle America and Mexico, and according to my own deep conviction, here in the United States, if our government can be persuaded to allow it.

I suggest as a parenthesis that, in ways less plainly sculptured, the identical proposition may hold good for the American Negro, the Japanese American, and the Puerto Rican. But this suggestion terminates in this parenthesis.

I commence my discussion of our Indian minority with a few items of general information about Indians, and then some information about the peculiarities of historical and present legal status, which demark the Indian status from that of our other minorities and which have been the occasions of violent fluctuations of public policy across more than one hundred years, down into this instant moment.

The Indians are Mongoloid migrants from Asia, whose first arrival was twenty thousand years ago, more or less. They occupied and used the whole of North and South America and of the Caribbean area. They developed, newly in the Western Hemisphere, languages numbering thousands; in the United States and Canada alone, the languages numbered some five hundred. N. A. Mc-Quown, in the *American Anthropologist* (June 1955), identifies two thousand languages and dialects from Northern Mexico southward. These Indian peoples achieved diversities of social organization almost matching the diversities of the whole pre-modern world. Almost universally, they had, and sustained into the period of white conquest, and even yet sustain, a world-view cooperative, not exploitative, toward nature, and actively tolerant toward the human multiplicities of difference. With a few famous exceptions (such as the Inca and in part the Aztec) they functioned democratically, with leadership of the permissive type, with action by what we know as the Quaker method, with a rather profound implicit or explicit realization of what we now call group dynamic principles, and with a symbolic, and what Laura Thompson calls a logico-aesthetic, profundity, equally found, for example, among hundreds of little tribes in California and in the Iroquois Confederation and in the Aztec and Inca dominions. Except for the Middle American nations, they remained preliterate, which does not mean that they had short memories or were historically shallow. By and large, the thousands of Indian cultural groups were made up of individuals group-disciplined and self-disciplined, but joyous, spontaneous, and out-giving. Unlike many of ourselves, they cared little about quantity and a great deal about quality; although here an exception might need to be made of the last phase of the huge Andean social-spiritual record, the 125 concluding years before white conquest.

The conventional assumption that innovation, invention, and change were strangers in ancient life—in preliterate, preindustrial, and primary group life—is exhaustively contradicted by the twenty-thousand-year Indian record. There took place inventions, innovations, and changes which numbered scores upon scores of thousands in languages, symbol systems, forms of gift-exchange and of trade, social systems, and craft and ecological and agricultural technologies. The conventional assumption, encountered in too many writings of educated men, is that the preoccupation of ancient man—specifically of American Indians—was with the enforcement of conformity; and in accepted and admirable sociological textbooks, we find the word "totalitarian" used to denote the so-called primitive or ancient life. The reality, written all over the Indian record at least, is a very different one. Limitation and canalization in human life are preconditions of freedom and creativity. Such they were with the Indians. Socially enriched and, therefore, self-disciplined, self-limiting personality, is (as we moderns sometimes forget) a precondition of freedom and creativity. Such it was with the Indians. If one wishes to think of statesmen, among Indians, he will think in Periclean rather than in Roman terms. The statesmen among the Indians were those who had achieved inner greatness, and who were concerned with public measures directed toward inner greatness in what we would call the individual citizen.

In this paper, such affirmations as are here made cannot be supported with the multitude of detail which exists; and the generalizations have to be broad, without the discussion of qualifying exceptions. I give the view of Indian life which was the view held by white men at earliest contacts, particularly in the United States and Canada, but also by such men as the Dominican monk, Las Casas. It was the view, again, of Frank H. Cushing and Alexander Hartley, and is the view of such contemporary or recent authorities as Felix S. Cohen, René d'Harnoncourt, J. M. B. Hewitt, Herbert J. Spinden, B. L. Whorf, Dorothy Lee, Laura Thompson, John G. Neihardt, Ward Shepard, and others whom I might name.

Before discussing the peculiarities of Indian status, particularly in the United States, I mention the demographic facts. I mean, here, the statistical numbers of Indians, reminding ourselves that the Jews who achieved so profoundly of old and who are achieving so profoundly now, were and are not numerous; that the Greeks who enabled Sir Henry Maine to remark that "All that moves in the modern world is Greek in its origin" were not numerous; that the creators of the shining and profound saga records in Iceland were just a handful of men. In history, the mere condition of bigness has borne but little relation to social, cultural, spiritual achievement.

The pre-conquest Indians may have numbered a maximum of a million and a half in what is now the United States and Canada: 15 million in Mexico and Central America; 16 million to 32 million within the Inca dominion, principally in the Andes; 30 million to 40 million in the Hemisphere. In 1940, according to estimates circulated by our Department of State, the Indians in North and South America numbered 30 million; the number today would be 40 million. Of this number, some 460,000 are in the United States and Alaska. Definitions are variable, but we may assume that the Indians today are hardly less numerous than the Indians of 1492; and they are one of the fastest-growing demographic or cultural groups within the Hemisphere.

I would again insist, however, that these data of quantities are not much more important in reality than they were in the consciousness of Indians of long ago. The Navajo tribe is seventy thousand in numbers; the Hopi pueblos are fewer than four thousand; but the Hopi cultural achievement, I believe, surpasses that of the Navajo. The famous and unsurpassed mimbres pottery achievement of the century before and after 1050 A.D., according to archaeological findings, was the product of some twenty to forty members of each generation (twenty to forty men and women) across six or seven generations. There can be experienced today, at Santo Domingo Pueblo, at Acoma Pueblo, among the Hopis, at Zuni Pueblo (to mention only a few examples very well known), a profundity, complexity, intensity, and versatility of cultural production that might not be exceeded even quantitatively in, for example, the whole of the Arab world or, one might suggest, in any one region of our cosmopolitan country. These thoughts are worth emphasizing because one of the facts which in popular and legislative thinking makes the United States Indians appear to be a vanishing race is the mere fact of their numerical fewness. How can an Indian society of two hundred souls or six hundred souls— how, to the quantity-minded thinker, can it hope to go on into the eons ahead? A mere law of social gravity must ensure its absorption and extinction. But groups as small as two hundred and six hundred, which were thousands of years old when the white man came, have transacted with the white man across four hundred and fifty years in the American Southwest and have not grown any bigger quantitatively through these late centuries, yet there they are, dynamic and magnetic functional realities, dependent on great personalities, and producing such personalities generation after generation. I do not suggest that they are going to go on through the eons, but only that their quantitative smallness will not be the reason why they die, if they die.

Now to the present—to the Indian as a resource and "problem" in the United States today and tomorrow. We shall find, however, that the Indian in the present, and governmental Indian policy, are intelligible and predictable, in large part, not otherwise than through an unextinguished history.

First, some broad facts. All Indians are full citizens of the United States. All have the franchise. All, in theory at least, have social security, which means a complex of federal and state relations. The majority of Indian children attend public schools along with their white neighbors, as they have done for nearly thirty years. The basic Indian populations continue, with some acceleration, to feed Indian blood into the general life-stream. Indian numbers increase rapidly, and the increase is greatest among the Indians not detribalized.

Now for the living history which explains and constitutes the Indian "problem" as somewhat different from the "problem" of any other ethnic group in our country.

I refer you to the standard book on federal Indian law, *The Handbook*, by Felix S. Cohen, a joint product of the Departments of Interior and Justice, a government publication of about 1940. Structurally, the situation in law and in the Indians' own mind has not greatly changed since *The Handbook* was completed.

The foundation of government-Indian relations is a contractual foundation. Indians were dealt with through treaties, Senate-ratified—bilateral compacts between European and Indian sovereignties. The treaty system, fully established in pre-Revolutionary years, was continued by the Union of the States. It was interpreted and elaborated through decisions of the Supreme Court and the lower courts. The treaties, still existent, number well above three hundred. So far as I know, the Indians have been loyal to the letter and spirit of the treaties. The executive and administrative branches have violated nearly all of these hundreds of compacts; but they have been reaffirmed by Congress, as of the present, to the extent that they are bases for the recovery of large sums, by tribes, from the government, on account of treaty violations by the government. And the principle of mutuality was reaffirmed by statute and in administrative practice, commencing in 1930 and 1933.

The treaties are, so to speak, the core of a body of court-elaborated and congressionally and administratively elaborated law and practice. The making of new treaties was ended by Congress eighty-five years ago; congressional-tribal agreements, i.e., compacts between tribes and both houses of Congress, were substituted.

Then, in 1934, in the Indian Reorganization Act, Congress reaffirmed and newly implemented the principle of bilateral mutual consent. Indians clothed themselves with the authorities of the Reorganization Act, or rejected these authorities, at tribal referenda pursuant to the Act. Those tribes (ultimately nearly eighty per cent of all the Indians) that came within the Reorganization Act then proceeded, usually, to organize their domestic home-rule and to incorporate for economic purposes, each of these political organizations and economic corporations being, in its turn, an affair of mutual compact between the government and the tribes. The Reorganization Act, among many other objectives, sought to make of the bilateral contractual relationship a living, evolving, and experimental relationship, mutual between the government and the tribes.

And administratively, those tribes which did not enact the Reorganization Act as their own law, identical authorities were conveyed by the government through administrative action. Thus, for example, the Navajo tribe, not under the Reorganization Act, exercises controls over its own affairs, political and economic, substantially identical with those which organized and incorporated tribes exercise under statutory authority.

Merely mentioned should be some enactments supplemental to the Reorganization Act. One was the Indian Arts and Crafts Board Act of 1933. One was the Johnson-O'Malley Act of the next year, empowering the Indian Service to establish cooperative relations, with supervised grants-in-aid, with local subdivisions of government and with social service and research organizations. The third was the Indian Claims Commission Act, formulated by Nathan R. Margold for the Brookings Institution before 1933, and finally enacted in 1946 after thirteen years of persuasion addressed to the Congress.

I emphasize that no one can deal intelligently with the resources and problems of the Indian, who ignores this ancient and living *bilateralism* of the government-Indian transaction. Repeatedly it has been ignored, across one hundred and twenty-five years. Congress ignored it, when decreeing that the many Indian tribes be forcibly removed west of the Mississippi. Congress and the Army denied or eluded the contractual relationship, generally throughout the country, with the resultant Indian wars which smoldered and blazed for more than ninety years—wars which, according to an Indian Commissioner's computation in 1865, cost the government a million dollars for every Indian killed. Again, Congress and the administration, with rationalized deliberation, denied the bilateral relationship, pursuant to the dictum of General Francis Walker, when he was Indian Commissioner in 1871:

When dealing with savage men as with savage beasts, no question of national honor can arise. Whether to fight, to employ a ruse, or to run away, is solely a question of expediency.

The general and special Allotment Acts, individualizing tribal properties, were unilateral and compulsory violations of the treaties. The long epoch of proselytization, largely compulsory, and of the treating of Indian religious devotions as criminal acts, was a denial of the bilateral relationship. Every one of these denials had effects disastrous for the individual Indian and his group, and was costly and unproductive for the United States government as well.*

But never was the philosophical continuity entirely forgotten or denied. The courts, almost unfailingly, adhered to the basic doc-

---

* Bilateralism, as Indian affairs policy, asserts a universal human-cultural condition, known to the ancients and re-revealed thousands of times over in cultural anthropology. This universal human-cultural condition is that human groups are in process of constant change (rapid or slow); that the change is due to stimuli or imperatives from outside the given group and also to the restless life-striving, the creativity, within the group; that in principle, the change-process in cultures and human groups is homologous with the change-process in biological organisms, and in ecological communities of earth, plants, and animals. The change-process is outward-reaching and inward-reaching (acculturative and enculturative, in the approximate usage of these two terms in anthropology); it is, when healthful and not lethal, a transacting two-way flow in all instances. Many missionaries, many makers of governmental policies, and quite too many academic minds, conceive that the two-way flow involves a self-contradiction, and that when public policy bases itself on the two-way-flow reality, it becomes unrealistic, impracticably idealistic, or "romantic." Such missionaries, makers of policies, and academicians are situated as were the philosophical absolutists, concept-dominated, as discussed by William James in his *A Pluralistic Universe*. An example is before me as I write this footnote, in a commentary by Robert A. Manners (*American Anthropologist*, p. 655, June 1955) on papers by Clyde Kluckhohn, Robert Hackenburg, myself, and others, delivered at the yearly meeting of the American Anthropological Association in December 1953. "Any program," writes Manners, "which tried to foster change without producing changes, and at the same time accepted the interdependence of cultural elements, would be foredoomed to schizophrenic inaction." Such, he implies, was (is) the Indian Reorganization Act program, or would be if the program were adhered to; such, one might add, would have been the Spanish Crown's Laws of the Indies as applied in Paraguay and in New Mexico; such would be the program of indirect administration of Britain, and most of the Point Four programs and of the technical assistance programs of United Nations. With seeming unawareness of the transactional thinking of Dewey, Bentley, Lewin, Paul Sears, Laura Thompson, and others, Mr. Manners appears as one of the many—not only some academicians, but those laymen in and out of Congress—who view as desirable or inevitable an ultimate cultural amorphousness or flatland, a one-way acculturation into no culture at all.

trines enunciated by John Marshall, i.e., that Indian grouphoods are cultural and practical sovereignties, withal, through historical events, inescapably dependent, in varying degrees, upon the federal government. Perhaps I can make the picture more understandable, through a case record.

The Spanish Laws of the Indies were made operative in New Granada—the American Southwest—after the Pueblo Rebellion of 1682. The Laws of the Indies, a product largely of that titanic Indian-Affairs reformer, Bartolomé de Las Casas, affirmed the overriding responsibility of the Crown for Indian welfare. They vested title to Indian tribes in parts or the entireties of their home lands. They acknowledged tribal and communal self-government. They were the beginnings of the system of indirect rule, in centuries long afterward elaborated by Britain and the Netherlands. The lamented late Felix S. Cohen has expounded the Spanish foundations of United States Indian law. But here, I concentrate on the Pueblos of New Mexico.

These pueblos, now numbering nineteen, speak four unrelated root languages. They are city-states, with cultures very rich, with institutions of discipline and of reciprocity that are complex and in part are obscure, and with embracing concentrations upon the personality development of their citizens.

In the middle 1850's, Calhoun, the first United States Indian Superintendent in New Mexico, negotiated treaties between the government and the pueblos. The treaties were never ratified, and they made no practical difference, because the treaties only restated that which had been Spanish policy and which had been taken over by the United States through the treaty of Guadalupe-Hidalgo with Mexico. The pueblos continued as self-governing, self-nurturing, peaceable and flowering, virtually autonomous social cultures.

But through the late years of Mexican rule, and all the early years of United States rule, encroachments by whites on the pueblo lands went forward, more or less with governmental consent. Then, about 1872, the Supreme Court, deviating from its earlier and subsequent records, decreed in the Joseph case that the federal-pueblo relationship existed no longer. The pueblo governments' own rulings had no force in law; individuals of the pueblo could sell out the communal properties. Thereupon, encroachments multiplied; a number of the pueblos were reduced to per capita subsistence levels, governmentally ascertained, of $14 and $16 a year. On their own part, the pueblos silently went ahead, asserting their way of life and exercising their legally interdicted authorities.

Then, in 1913, Justice Van Derventer departed from the Supreme Court rooms and consulted the Smithsonian Institution. There ensued a unanimous decision of the Supreme Court, known as the Sandoval Decision, which completely reversed the earlier, Joseph Decision of 1872. The Sandoval Decision reaffirmed the existence of the bilateral relationship, and struck the foundations from under the claims of all of the thousands who had encroached on the pueblo lands and waters.

Meantime, however, administrative pressures, aimed at the dissolution of pueblo authority and spirit, went ahead unabated. Forcible land allotment was placed on some of the southwestern tribes, and was attempted across twelve years among the Hopi pueblos of Arizona. The stated objective of the government schools was "to break up the pueblo."

Then, in 1921–1923, under Albert B. Fall as Secretary of the Interior, a bill was introduced, and was passed in the Senate, whose broad effect was to validate all "squatter" claims against the pueblos' lands and waters, and to bring the secret disciplines and religious faiths of the pueblos into common inspection through court actions. Thus commenced the most determined and, until 1950, the most recent, effort at the tribal destruction of Indians. For the Indian Bureau's efforts at the killing of Indian life extended beyond the pueblos to all the tribes, and the Indian Omnibus Bill of 1923, which passed the House and was killed on the Senate floor by the elder LaFollette, presented itself as the full-blown precursor of legislation introduced and partly enacted under the present administration. By intent, it overrode exhaustively all bilateral commitments, totally individualized the Indian properties, and totally sought the effacement of the Indian from the American universe.

Now, turning for a moment to the Indians' response—specifically the pueblos' response. There was "brought alive," after two and a half centuries, the Council of All the New Mexico Pueblos.

This Council, like the individual pueblos, adhered usually to the unanimity principle in its actions. It sent to many parts of the country, and to Washington, adequate representatives of the Indians' own case. It or its city-state members conducted across more than eleven years difficult lawsuits, aimed at the recovery of usurped lands or of compensation for lands not recovered. It resisted, through Gandhian modes of resistance, the government's effort to forbid the initiation of Indian youths into Indian religious disciplines and consecrations. It paid no attention to the Indian Bureau's announcement that these un-American activities were financed from Soviet Moscow, and no more attention to the allegation that these Indian peoples, one hundred per cent Christian, were whipping their individuals into paganism. The pueblos waged their battle in no angry, but in a genial spirit, not against the government alone, but against the ubiquitous missionaries and their bishops. The Catholic Church is excepted from this statement.

Meantime, the Supreme Court reaffirmed and extended, and wrote out in detail, those earlier findings, mentioned as the Sandoval Decision of 1913. The pueblos, the Court held, were municipal corporations, clothed with authorities which existed before any white ruler came, which had been reaffirmed by all the white rulers, and which were unextinguishable save only through an explicit act of Congress. (The power of Congress, in matters concerning and derived from treaties, is, of course, plenary, as the Supreme Court had acknowledged when the Cherokees of Oklahoma appealed to the Court against the forced allotment of their lands. In the division of powers, within our government, in relation to Indian matters at least, the authority of Congress has been and remains in practical effect plenary—unconditioned and substantially extraconstitutional. This state of affairs the Courts cannot mend; only the citizenry can mend it.)

The pueblos' struggles were duplicated in multiform ways by Indian groups all over the United States, and there emerged an Indian-formulated restatement of the bilateral concept. The main principles of the Indian Reorganization Act had been formulated in Indian minds—not the pueblo mind alone but the minds of many tribes, including Alaskan groups—in the years before the Indian

Reorganization Act was passed in 1934. The Indian New Deal of the Franklin Roosevelt administration was in its central principles Indian-made, and appears both as an Indian New Deal and a re-implementation of the fundamental understandings between the Indians and the United States, which were and are the system of Indian law and the norm of Indian action.

I must now try to answer the question which will be in each of your thoughtful minds.

Is the historical continuum, in fundamental law and in the Indian mind—that is, the principle of mutual consent or bilateralism in public policy toward Indians—practicable now and for the future?

And even if theoretically or ideally practicable as well as being the honorable, democratic, and creative way, is it a principle which can be applied and developed within the system of Congressional near-absolutism, and bureaucratic tendencies toward the imposition of blueprints, toward regimentation, toward the proclaimed or tacitly implied authoritarianism of government?

My attempted answer will not be dogmatic—it could not be, in the light of the condition of Indian Affairs since the year 1950.

However, I do invite attention to some processes and achievements that are, at the least, suggestive of a certain proposition. That proposition is that the bilateralism, imperfectly achieved in Indian affairs, may be identified as predictive of desirable futures all over the world, rather than as a historical vestige.

One reference would be to that system which is called indirect rule or indirect administration, a fundamental of British colonial policy since its beginnings were made in Nigeria and Fiji two generations ago. It was the Netherlands' principle in Indonesian rule, independently developed at about the same time that British indirect rule became formulated. The essence of indirect rule is mutual consent between the ruling power and the "dependent" group. In indirect administration, events are composite or integrative—the purposes and necessities of the ruling group and the purposes and necessities of the dependent group are united into one flow, through cumulative empirical endeavor by both sides. The success of indirect administration has been uneven, extending all the way from the mere "cushioning" of European impact upon dependent peoples to the release of great and practicable energies among the dependent peoples. Fiji, the Gold Coast, recent Western Samoa, the Anchau Corridor or Nigeria are examples of success. In this paper there is no room for expanding on indirect administration, beyond pointing out that it furnishes not merely an analogy but a homology, i.e., identity of principle and structure, with the enterprise of bilateralism in Indian affairs.

Are there analogies or homologies closer home? I believe that the answer is "Yes." The Tennessee Valley Authority, in its myriad phase of community development, is not an authority at all; it is a procedure under mutual agreements. The more than three thousand Soil Conservation Districts, which are new organs of government, are clothed with almost no authority; and the tens of thousands of actions which are changing the face of the land from the Pacific to the Atlantic, in the Soil Conservation Districts, are voluntary action ultimately between the Soil Conservation technician and the individual land user, within the framework of watershed-wide democratic planning. I suggest that the T.V.A. and the Soil Conservation Districts, while they do incorporate the grass-roots, town-meeting, and independent pioneering principles, also are outreachings toward modes of public action—of governmental action—which are of the possible future even more than of the past.

I make another reference, this time to the now fast-multiplying experiences in the cooperative development of so-called underdeveloped peoples. It is by now an accepted fact that the developmental processes, which we in the United States have come to know as Point Four technical aid enterprises, are successful, and also are uncostly, in a rather exact ratio to the non-use of authority, the blending of technical assistance with community self-help, the multiplication of varieties of development, and, in general, bilateralism.

One might be tempted to give examples from industry—not only the worldwide distributive cooperative movement, but such a case as that of the McCormick Industry centering at Baltimore, where, be it an active, conscious consent to suggestion from management or be it experimental innovation by the rank and file, the flow of decision and authority is from the local societies, and from the different levels of industrial employment, toward the summit, and not from the summit toward the lower levels and the local societies. Even, as in the McCormick Industry, the principle of unanimity of consent has been found to be impressively productive, in terms of morale and of increased practical efficiency, in a competitive field of industry.

And as a final, merely suggestive remark, I remind us of the philosophy of John Dewey, and even more, of Kurt Lewin, and of so-called patient-centered therapy, and of the somewhat revolutionary insights that are emerging in that region of experimentation which we now call group dynamics and social action research.

These suggestions, left so general, will have to appear cloudy. I pass to the Indian Reorganization Act, and to some of the ways in which it made of bilateralism a practicable mode of government-Indian relations. Thoroughly practicable, that is, so long as pressure groups were held at bay and the United States government was willing to take the trouble, which means for nearly twenty years.

1. As stated earlier in this paper, the Act itself became operative, initially, solely through a majority vote by the men and women of any given tribe, at a formal referendum. I should add that questionnaires designed to focus thinking toward the formulation of a new organic act had been addressed to all Indian tribes in 1933. And the prolonged Congressional hearings on the Reorganization bill were suspended, to allow, and to give attention to, the discussion of the Reorganization bill by the Indians at conferences held in many parts of the United States.

2. Any tribe which adopted the Act obligated itself to conserve its natural resources, particularly its biological resources. That feature of the Act caused its rejection by the Navajo tribe by a majority of a few hundred.

3. All land allotment directives, statutory or administrative, were annulled for those tribes which made the Act their own. This meant that the atomization of the properties of the tribe was brought to an end.

4. A tribe that adopted the Act was then empowered, but not required, to organize under a charter of home rule. The charter became effective upon approval of the Secretary of the Interior,

but was not revocable or amendable by him, but only by the tribe or by Congress.

5. Similarly, the tribe was empowered but not required to organize itself into a corporation for economic enterprises. The corporate charter became effective when approved by the Secretary of the Interior, but could not be revoked or amended by him.

6. Among the authorities vested through the tribal constitution and the charter, was the authority on the part of the tribes to enter into cooperative arrangements with local divisions of government or appropriate federal divisions or private scientific or service organizations. The control of tribally owned funds was, substantially, vested in the organized tribe, as it had been, one or two years earlier, in the case of the New Mexico pueblos.

7. The inadequacy of the Indians' *resources base* was declared, and appropriations of $2,000,000 a year for the purchase of new lands, in behalf of the tribes, were authorized. With the use of various funds and authorities, the Indian land base was extended from about fifty-two million acres to more than fifty-six million acres in the ensuing ten years. Alongside this increase in quantity of lands, the Act contemplated consolidation, through voluntary group and individual Indian actions, of the fractionated allotments and heirship equities. Such consolidation has been achieved in varying measures, from a few per cent of the needed total to one hundred per cent, the second being true of the voluntary return to common ownership of all allotted lands by the individual members of the Jicarilla Apache tribe.

8. Ownership of properties by Indians is not enough. Their utilization by the owners is more important. Before the Reorganization Act, merely as an example, the four Apache tribes in New Mexico and Arizona owned areas of land which were adequate, but leased them to whites. Through the use of the Reorganization Act, all of these tribes have resumed the control and operation of all of their lands, applying at the same time principles of conservation to their whole estates. The change of social climate within these tribes is not less striking than the increase of their economic production and the proliferation of their cooperative enterprises. From social vacuum to social abundance, these tribes have moved.

9. A revolving loan fund was authorized and appropriated; loans repaid by the tribe or its members were reapplicable to the tribe and its members. The revolving loan system was then developed through a great number of joint actions by the Indian Service and the tribes, the controlling principle being the submission of economic plans by the borrower and their approval by the tribal credit organization.

Previous credit, totaling millions, to Indians had been a notoriously scandalous waste and failure, not resulting in much increase of capital goods, and with a permanent delinquency rate of more than sixty per cent. Under the Reorganization Act system, the Indian immediately demonstrated himself as almost or quite the best credit risk in the country. Up to 1950, the totals loaned or reloaned were some $25,000,000 and the losses, charged off, were some $60,000.

10. The creation of an Indian Civil Service was directed by the Act. Indians, equally, though as a rule differently, qualified, as compared to white job-seekers, were given preference. This clause of the Act was never fully implemented, but Indians became numerous and successful at all levels of Indian Service employment, including the administrative and, in so far as practicable, technical.

11. The Indians' need for education at colleges and universities was declared, and $250,000 a year was authorized toward meeting this need.

This overcondensed summary of the Reorganization Act and its consequences may be supplemented by a quotation from Professor Laura Thompson's book, *Personality and Government*, published in 1951, that book being a summarization of the results of the Indian Personality and Administration Research, a cooperative interdisciplinary enterprise that went forward for nearly ten years after 1941:

(1) Three-fourths of the Indians in the United States and Alaska have accepted reorganization; one hundred tribes have adopted their own constitutions for local self-government and almost 200 tribal economic organizations have been formed; . . . (3) stocking on overstocked Indian range lands has been systematically reduced to the scientific estimates of the range-carrying capacity on most Indian reservations, while Indian beef cattle holdings have increased 105

per cent in number of head and 2,300 per cent in yield of animal products; (4) agricultural production on Indian reservations has multiplied fourfold; (5) about 60 per cent of the employees in the Indian Service are Indians; (6) a beginning has been made toward creating machinery for the just settlement of Indian tribal claims; (7) the federal Indian school system has been reorganized toward greater practicality and community usefulness; (8) scientific research yielding findings of critical and universal significance has been conducted in the areas of soil and wild life conservation, health, genetics, law, social organization, personality, linguistics, in-service training and community administration; (9) the Indian death rate has decreased 55 per cent in fourteen years and the Indians of the United States, now far from a vanishing race, are increasing at a rate of about 1.2 per cent a year.

The consistent voluntarism and the manifold bilateralism of the Act and of the procedures under it are its outstanding feature. The results were as important psychologically as materially. An impressive increase of Indian social energy took place; and in Indian Service, experimentalism, empirical adventurousness, and creativity became rather usual. This state of affairs, within the government service, continued until 1950, and among the Indians it continues, quite undiminished, in the face of legislative and administrative attempts at suppression.

Across seventeen years, the newly implemented, ancient bilateralism of Indian-government relations went on elaborating itself; and then came the Dillon S. Myer administration in 1950.

To Dillon Myer, the existence of all that I have described appeared undesirable and, one must assume, in some scarcely formulated way un-American. Myer perceived the Indian communities, and the government's Indian Affairs system, as being homologous with the War Relocation system under which 105,000 Japanese Americans had been cruelly interned during the Second World War. He applied himself administratively to the breakup of the whole bilateral construction, and he propagandized Congress toward that end.

Then came the Eisenhower administration, and the extremely hurried enactment, without adequate hearings or any hearings, of a series of bills which were deliberate violators of treaty and compact, and which contemplated, or achieved, a return to the atomizing policies of the years before 1928. The most sweeping of these enactments, Public Law 280 (1953), signed by President Eisenhower with a lamentation, authorized any local state government to replace the federal government, in the essentials of Indian matters, by itself, wholly upon its own initiative, and to displace also the tribal governments. Another enactment, striking at isolated and poor Indian groups in Utah, declared in effect that inasmuch as they had not received what was coming to them of federal protection and aid heretofore, they could not have it hereafter. The most massive of the enactments dissolved the governmental-tribal operations on the great Klamath Reservation of Oregon, terminated the perpetual-yield administration of the Klamath forest, authorized any individual member of the tribe to compel the tribe to sell its common assets and buy him out; and generally, destroyed, or is pointed to destroy, an economic operation on which the whole Klamath Basin is dependent.

This paper already has exceeded its practicable limits, so that I do not specify any others of the administrative and legislative assaults against the Indians, which were at their most intense, legislatively speaking, through 1954, and are now checked momentarily through the shift of control of the House and Senate. The *administrative* assaults go forward unchecked and uncriticized except by the Indians, almost unanimously, and by the Indian Rights and Indian Welfare groups, I believe unanimously.

Is there an ideology behind the present administration's drive against Indian social life? The ideology or prepossession seems to be, merely, that cultural and social distinctiveness is offensive, and is contrary to the American way—an extreme oversimplification of the American melting-pot hypothesis or stereotype.

In the process of "liquidating" or "withdrawing" the Indian Service, the appropriations for Indian Service have been increased threefold in five years. Historically, the situation is rather precisely identifiable with the situation of 1890 and 1900 and, again, of 1917 and 1922–1924. Now as then, the government, departing unashamedly from its historical role, defying its contractual obligations and ignoring prior experience, is seeking to disinherit the Indians materially and culturally, and to force upon them the dubious boon of "anomie"—of homelessness, grouplessness, and guidelessness. The previous "drives" of this character have hurt the Indians but not destroyed them, have suspended the national commitment but not permanently annulled it; and observing Indian life, and going among Indians and witnessing their political actions, in the year 1955, thoughtful observers feel rather well assured that the Indians are not going to yield in their own wills, or to be effaced, through a renewal of intermittent ancient pressures toward a kind of social, cultural, spiritual self-genocide. Not only the covert part of Indian life is living on ("covert" being a word familiar to anthropologists), but the overt, conscious, systematized, group-directed, and individually impelled striving of the Indians, to hold fast that which is good, appears to be at a higher level now than it ever was since the white man came. So the final verdict is not yet in.

But I asked, earlier in this paper, a different question. Acknowledging that the way of bilateralism, in Indian and in wider human affairs, is the efficient, productive, and economical way as well as being a democratic obligation; yet, can one hope that the Congress and the bureaucracy will resume that way, and be faithful to it hereafter? If the answer be one of despair—and certainly, much evidence of the remoter past, and of the instant present, intimates despair—then I suggest that the despair must reach far beyond Indians. It must be a despair about the survival of any ever-self-renewing democracy in our national life; a despair about anything prevailing except pressure-group controls, public administration stereotypes, and mere wind-herdedness of national electorates. Most of us will not—we will not yet—embrace a despair so life-denying as that. It is our business to refute the despair.

Commentary

THEODORE H. HAAS [*]

I do not share the note of pessimism which permeates the last part of Professor Collier's paper. I admit that during the dozen years

---

[*] Because of illness, John Collier was unable to be present at this Institute session. However, his paper was read by Mr. Haas and then supplemented by these remarks.

of his Commissionership of Indian Affairs (1933–1945), the zenith was attained both of bilateralism and the reinvigoration of Indian grouphood. Moreover, for the first time since the rediscovery of America by Columbus the Indian land base was increased.

In 1955 there are, however, several bright spots in Indian administration which illuminate my prognosis of the Indians' future. In 1954 six laws were enacted by Congress providing for the termination of Federal supervision of certain groups totaling some eight thousand Indians. But there has been a pause in its implementation of House Committee Resolution 108, 82nd Congress, which had spawned the policy of rapid termination. The Indian Bureau and the Congress seem to realize that much damage would result if Indian groups are placed on their own before they prepared themselves adequately, with the aid of the Bureau and other agencies. Moreover, since the issuance of the epoch-making report of Meriam and associates in 1928, great strides have been taken by most Indians in every important field: education, health, economic development, civil rights, and organization. An important vehicle for this progress was the Johnson-O'Malley Act of April 16, 1934 (48 Stat. 596), which has enabled state and local governments to play an increasingly major role in Indian affairs.

As a result of an emergency education program, 1954–1955, there is now a desk for every Navaho child of school age in a school of some kind—Indian boarding or day school or trailer, public or mission school. On April 19, 1950, when the Navaho-Hopi Rehabilitation Act (64 Stat. 44), was enacted, fifteen thousand Navaho children lacked schools and teachers. Today, there are educational facilities for practically all Indian children of school age. Aided perhaps by an adult education program just started for five tribal groups, the illiteracy rate of almost one Indian in three will soon be reduced markedly.

Another hopeful sign is that the Public Health Service, to which Indian health activities were transferred on July 1, 1955, is expanding to meet the acute health needs of the Indians. The task facing the Service is tough. According to Dr. James Shaw, Chief of the Indian Health Division, in 1950 the average age of the Indians at death was thirty-six years, in contrast to sixty-one years for the white population. The death rate of Indians from preventable diseases, such as measles, tuberculosis, pneumonia, influenza, and typhoid fever is several times that of the rest of the population. Malnutrition, dental decay, uncorrected physical defects, blindness, and loss of hearing—all contribute to the burden on the individual Indian and his family and on the nation as a whole.

The Government's program to improve the health of the Indians was one of the earliest public health programs. As early as 1832, the Congress authorized the Secretary of War, who was then in charge of Indian affairs, to provide for the vaccination of Indians against smallpox. A century and a quarter later, the Public Health Service, Indian Health Division, operates the largest number of small hospitals of any Government agency—about fifty hospitals with a total bed capacity of about four thousand, including a few large, modern ones. Contracts are also being made increasingly with private hospitals and local governmental facilities.

There has been some notable research conducted by Federal doctors engaged in Indian health work. Dr. Loe discovered a cure for trachoma, an eye disease which brought blindness to many Indians, and Dr. Aronsen demonstrated the effectiveness of the B.C.G. vaccine in reducing the rate of tuberculosis among some Indian groups.

In the last two years, appropriations for Indian health service have been doubled, thus enabling the application for the first time of large-scale disease prevention work. Indian families on the reservations are receiving advice and guidance on the construction and maintenance of safe water supplies, the disposal of garbage, the control of insect-breeding places, and on many other phases of personal and community health protection. In this way, health educators and sanitary engineers, assisted by community workers, are seeking to reduce Indian disease and death rates to the level of the general population in 1955. The existing rate is comparable to that of the general population fifty years ago.

This goal, however, cannot be accomplished unless the low economic base of most Indians is drastically raised. In fact, the making of a decent living is a key problem around which revolve most of the other problems, including education, health, and housing. Since 1929, when President Hoover sent a special message to the Congress seeking additional appropriations for Indian health, education, and economic development, the per capita income of most Indians has increased many times—even to a larger degree than that of the general population. The report of the Commissioner of Indian Affairs for 1946 stated that the agricultural income per Indian family in twenty-five Indian reserves increased from $313 to $1,526. Since most Indians derive their main income from the production of food, as farmers, ranchers, or fishermen, it has declined in recent years. This decline is all the more serious because the Indian population is increasing at the rate of one per cent per annum, and, at the same time, their land resources are decreasing. It is, therefore, necessary for many thousands of Indians each year to leave the reservations.

On September 20, 1948, in an address to a conference of the field staff of the Extension Division of the Indian Bureau at Billings, Montana, I said, in part, as follows:

> Since an objective of the Bureau is to assist Indians to become self-sufficient, I believe that assistance in relocating and securing permanent off-reservation employment, will continue to grow in importance, eventually becoming the principal work of the Indian Bureau. I predict that within the next few years the placement work which has begun at the Navaho will be extended to many of the reservations. Not only is it important to secure jobs but also such important things as community acceptance, housing, perhaps temporary shelters or hostels at the beginning, and the cooperation and assistance of governmental and private organizations, and citizens. Of course, relocation must be voluntary and some of the Indians will desire to cling to their Indian way of life. Nevertheless, save for periods of depression when some will return, the flow of Indians from the reservations will be practically continuous.

This prophecy has been partly fulfilled. While at the beginning of the program the relocatees may represent merely a trickle of a few thousand each year, the program is expected to gather momentum. It is interesting to note that the Los Angeles and Chicago industrial areas that contain the largest population of Japanese Americans have been the most popular regions for the relocation of Indians.

This brings me to one of the main fears in Professor Collier's paper, namely, that Indian organization and the Indian way of life are threatened with extinction. It is remarkable that so much of

Indian tradition and culture has survived so long. In part, in my opinion, the durability of Indian traits in some groups has been aided by misguided Government programs to compel them to fit into a common mold made by the United States which increased rather than decreased the desire of these Indians to remain separate.

The creed of the United States is that everyone is entitled to practice the culture of his group and also, if he wishes, to participate in part or all of the cultural life of the dominant group. Thus, although Indian groups may borrow many techniques of the industrial age, they may retain many of their ancient customs and traditions which they still find meaningful. To cite two random examples, many members of the Eastern Cherokee Band of North Carolina, and of the Sac and Fox Indians of Iowa lost something which was essential, they felt, to the continuance of their grouphood—their lands. Impoverished as each group was, they each managed to purchase some more land and to continue their tribal organization.

But even under this more enlightened policy the pressures for conformity and the lures of modern living, the radio, the auto, the television, etc., are speeding up the pace of acculturation. The increasing regimentation of our atomic age is reaching even some of the most isolated regions. Indian groups which resisted exile, forced relocation, dispersal, and the cannons and guns of invaders with big canoes and still retained their Indianness are in many cases split widely on the question of how much of the western culture should be absorbed by them. Even fairly solid groups like the Zunis, the Navahos, and the Hopis that have retained much of their land, religious traditions, and ways of life are finding that the cultural conflict between the old and new generation is becoming more intense. The sharp cleavage between the branch of certain Hopi villages known as the traditionalists, and the other branch known as the progressive groups, illustrates this chasm.

Assistant Commissioner Thomas M. Reid and Program Officers Joe Jennings and Graham Holmes spent the last two weeks of July, 1955, seeking to learn how the Government can assist the twelve Hopi villages which have retained some of their pre-Columbian culture. On the first day, one of the Hopi leaders, Dan Katchongra, said, in part:

Many of the people followed a new life of the White man and tried to influence many of our people who are following their own way of life, and it seems it is a great struggle now between these people who want to follow their own way of life and those people who have broken away from the life pattern and accepted these many policies of the White man.

He and other traditionalists among the Hopi stated that they are fearful that a new plan of the Government will result in the loss of their land, traditions, and religious beliefs.

I agree with Professor Collier that the Hopi and other Indian groups should be permitted to retain without fear the spiritual and materialistic portions of their culture. However, it is clear that many of them seek a new way of life.

In passing, let me note that while I agree also that small groups of people can maintain and have maintained a great culture, some modern conveniences require a complex industrial and technological society. Such a society has flourished only in countries with large urban centers.

Finally, the thousands of Indians who are relinquishing their old way of life comprise some of the most acculturated of the Indians. Affording them opportunities for making a livelihood elsewhere constitutes a safety valve for Indian communities which desire to continue to maintain their ancient ways of life. The coming of Indians to cities constitutes a challenge to urban dwellers and local and state governments. Fortunately, since 1924, when all Indians born in the United States became citizens of the nation and the state of their residence, in most places discriminations against Indians have been eliminated—no more disenfranchisement, nonpayment of social security benefits, and inability to sue the United States for violation of treaties, and other unfair dealings, without special legislation. Hence, relocatees are in a better position than ever to make a successful adjustment.

The gains in Indian affairs have been due in no small measure to an awakening conscience and to an understanding of Indian affairs on the part of an increasing segment of the public. This development has been manifested during 1955 by the formation of thousands of study groups on Indians by church women. Moreover, the historic pronouncement of the General Board of the National Council of Churches on March 3, 1955, recognizes "the necessity for assuring to each tribe or band the right to preserve to the extent consistent with the general welfare, its own cultural identity." This statement exemplifies also the way in which America has been and can continue to be enriched "by the Indian cultural heritage." With this increasing appreciation of the importance of Indians in our national life, their future is brighter than has been portrayed.

CHAPTER IV

The American Jew

OSCAR HANDLIN*

$\mathbb{A}$ discussion of the group must begin with some description of its character. Yet such a description is difficult to present
in the absence of reliable statistics or an accepted definition of the
group. Its complexity, diversity, and variety defy a neat categor-
ization in terms of origin, status, or even of religious affiliation.
The most that can be said is that the Jews of America today constitute a group loosely held together by a consciousness of com-
mon elements of tradition, experience, and antecedents. |In part,
their cohesion springs from the recollection of a long religious
tradition that some of them have abandoned but that nevertheless
has left its mark upon their ideas and their way of life; in part it
springs from the history of their settlement in the United States.
In any event, these people significantly act as an ethnic group and
may intelligibly be discussed as such.

The character of the American Jews as a group can therefore

be understood only in the light of its adjustment and development within the American context. However important may be the qualities derived from the traditions of two thousand years of history before 1654, they affected the group's development within the specific terms of the New World environment. The American adjustment passed through three distinct chronological phases; and a description of those phases is the main subject of this paper.

The first phase, and the longest, extended from the origins of settlement in the seventeenth century to the end of the nineteenth century. It was dominated by the general problems of expansion and immigration adjustment; through these years, at any given time, the foreign-born constituted a majority of the Jews in the United States.

It is difficult, of course, to speak generally of a period that covered so long an extent of time and comprehended a variety of conditions both in the nation and in the group itself. In these two hundred and fifty years, a handful of settlements along the edge of the Atlantic Ocean grew to become a great industrial power covering the continent to the Pacific. The number of Jews sprang from the scattering of arrivals in 1654 to a group that numbered in the millions in 1900. Nevertheless, despite important diversities in the patterns of settlement and adjustment, it is possible to discern certain significant general trends, particularly such as concerned the relationship of the evolving community to immigration.

That relationship conditioned the character of American Jews through most of the period. By the end of the nineteenth century it was certainly possible to describe the life of the group in terms of well-developed communal organizations. But at that point it was also necessary to distinguish two separate and distinct Jewish communities in the United States within which the life of individual Jews was organized. The two existed side by side with each other, but maintained few meaningful contacts with one another.

On the one hand there was a community generally referred to as that of the German Jews. Immigrants from Germany and their children formed an important, but by no means the only, element in this community, which included also Jews from other parts of Europe. More important than the place of origin of its members was the general orientation of this community toward the values of

Western Europe and particularly of Germany. The ideals of the enlightenment and of emancipation shaped its intellectual and social outlook, and therefore also its organizational forms. \These people did not consider it their destiny to stand permanently apart as a nation; rather they conceived that they would increasingly approach other Americans except in religious affiliation. Appropriately enough, therefore, the central concerns of their communal life, aside from the support of facilities for worship, were philanthropic. The community was already well developed before 1880 and had by that time brought into existence a complex of religious, cultural, charitable, and fraternal associations that gave it formal structure.

Existing side by side with it was an entirely different community of Eastern European Jews, largely the product of the immigration of the last two decades of the nineteenth century. This community would continue to grow in numbers after the turn of the century and until the end of the period of free immigration in 1924.

It was, in 1900, already internally divided; and that division would persist long into the twentieth century. On the one hand, it was influenced by Eastern European Jewish life. The great mass of immigrants had been Orthodox at home and, in migration, attempted to preserve the forms of their Orthodoxy. In modes of religious worship, in habits of behavior, even in diet, there was a persistent attractiveness to the familiar and the traditional. On the other hand these forms were difficult to maintain in the New World; they had already begun to disintegrate even in the Old; and there was no Orthodox leadership—lay or clerical—to offer guidance to the problems of adjustment.

Therefore the Eastern European Jewish community was profoundly influenced by the radical labor leadership, impatient for a change in many aspects of society. The stream of migration had brought along with the Orthodox masses a small but influential group of intellectuals and dissidents, embittered by their experience at home and persuaded that a total reconstruction of society was necessary. Often they were Socialists; but even if they were not, they were impressed with the necessity of improving the lot of the laborers among whom the great majority of the newcomers found themselves. They offered leadership where none other was available, spoke the same language and sprang from the same background as the common folk, and enjoyed the inestimable advantage of a sympathetic understanding of the situation in which the immigrants found themselves. Their following grew steadily through the years among the readers of the New York *Forward*, among the members of the unions in the needle trades, and among the voters for the Socialist party.

Between the radicals, distrustful of tradition and eager for change, and the Orthodox there were often bitter conflicts. Yet the two groups nevertheless constituted a single community. They shared a common institutional development, spoke the same language—Yiddish—were members of the same fraternal associations, and often were drawn together by family ties. These links supplied a basis for common action, despite the struggle for leadership and for control of the direction action would take.

From this point of view, both the Orthodox and the radicals were then decisively set apart from the older community of German Jews. There were occasional, but infrequent, points of contact between the two. The well-established "Germans," for instance, accepted the obligation to aid their newly arrived coreligionists. But this was aid from outsiders. There was very little that was shared in their experience. The differences in the time and manner of immigration had left the two communities separate.

After 1900, the immigrant institutions continued to function and, indeed, grew in number and size. The expansion of their activities was in part due to the fact that immigration increased in volume until it was interrupted by war in 1914 and cut off by law in 1924. In addition, the organizations themselves had by then acquired a stable form that permitted them to serve an important role in the lives of their members, even after the original needs that had called them into being disappeared.

But after 1900, such associations receded steadily in relative importance in the concerns of American Jews. New developments overshadowed the problems of immigration; and in the process, they both weakened the two old communities and, at the same time, by establishing more frequent points of contact between them, began to create an area of common interest for all Jews in the United States. Five factors that made themselves felt after the turn of the century were responsible.

ʿThe first was the increasing pressure for overseas aid from 1905 onward. Earlier crises had evoked action by American Jews even in the nineteenth century. But the new problems were of a magnitude so much greater than before as to constitute a prolonged challenge to the existing forms of communal organization.

The Jews of Europe had entered upon a period of profound instability that would reach its climax in the last years of the First World War and would extend on into the decade of the 1920's. They had become the targets of political animus and outright persecution, and the basis of their economic position was steadily being eroded. In this situation, Americans could not stand idly by.

The first disturbances came in the violence of the pogroms. Aid was therefore at first conceived as a protest against persecutions encouraged or tolerated by the governments of Russia and Romania. It was thus, to begin with, political; and it depended for success on the ability to mobilize broad sectors of public opinion.

But aid was also, of necessity, in part economic. The victims of persecution needed relief in reconstructing their lives, and often saw no future for themselves but emigration, which depended for success on the help of outsiders. Earlier philanthropic efforts of this sort now became continuous. The First World War and its aftermath heightened the sense of urgency. These disturbances upset millions of Jews in Central and Eastern Europe and created immediate problems of relief to the destitute as well as long-term problems of reconstruction for the displaced. Furthermore, the old established Jews in Germany and Western Europe were themselves hard hit by the war and the leadership in these endeavors passed into the hands of their American coreligionists.

The pressure for overseas aid tended to draw the two American Jewish communities together. Both the necessity of arousing opinion in the interests of the victims of persecution and the necessity of collecting funds for their rehabilitation created interests common to all American Jews. The earlier misunderstandings and antagonisms did not at once disappear. But the plight of those who needed help was a potent inducement toward cooperation among all groups in the United States. The growing rapprochement did not dissolve all differences; nor did it create over-all organizational unity. But the differences that persisted thereafter were more often based upon ideological and social considerations than upon "national origins." That is, divisions were less likely to occur between the "Germans" as such and the "Russians" as such, and were more likely to occur over the objectives and tactics of relief. Furthermore, they came within a fresh sense of community that developed from working together toward the solution of common problems.

A second factor that tended to develop the same sense of community was the necessity for defense against the rising anti-Semitic movements in the United States. These movements originated in the first decade of the nineteenth century, then grew steadily in importance to the First World War and the years immediately thereafter. In the 1920's, animus toward the Jews was a prominent element in the program of the Ku Klux Klan; that organization and its sympathizers diffused through the United States the frightening conception of an international conspiracy of Jews to rule the world. Anti-Semitism expressed itself directly in the pattern of discrimination in employment and education that limited the opportunities of Jews and it threatened also, by attacking their civic rights, to make them thoroughly insecure in the United States.

The response on the part of Jews was the formation of a number of "defense" organizations dedicated to the purpose of refuting the charges of anti-Semitic agitators, of educating Americans as to the character of the Jews, and of resisting any efforts to restrict civic or political rights. The American Jewish Committee, established in 1906, was the first to set itself to these tasks, but it by no means held the field to itself. Again, the real differences did not at once disappear and no single central organization united all Jews. But none could blink at the fact that the anti-Semites attacked alike the German and the East European, the banker and the labor leader, the Orthodox and the Reformed. Certainly the sense of common danger stimulated the feeling of community, whatever real divergencies remained as to programs and methods of defense.

The end of the period of free immigration was a third factor operating in the same direction. So long as a constant stream of newcomers kept arriving in the United States, they added force to the divisions based upon the differences in the backgrounds whence they originated. They also maintained a continuity of contact with the Old World that strengthened those differences. The decline of immigration necessarily weakened all such influences. After 1920, the percentage of the foreign-born among American Jews declined steadily and leadership moved noticeably into the hands of the native-born. There remained differences between the children of the "Russians" and those of the "Germans," but they shared also the experience of education and of life in the New World. That common experience also tended to increase the area of community within which all could act together.

A fourth factor appeared in the 1930's as a result of the acute crisis in which American Jews then found themselves. The whole nation in that decade seemed at the verge of social catastrophe. A prolonged depression kept millions of men out of work for long periods and rendered every social relationship unstable. Jews were particularly affected, because many of them were in marginal occupational groups hard hit by the slackening of economic expansion. Furthermore they felt the ominous threat of the increased potential for anti-Semitism. Social and economic disorder were the ground in which group antagonisms of every sort bred; and there were fears that those antagonisms might convert the pattern of discrimination—already burdensome—into some more overt form of hostility to the Jews. A number of blatant anti-Semitic movements with substantial memberships was evidence that there was some substance to these fears.

The events in Europe in that decade added still more evidence, if that was needed. The advent of Hitler to power shattered the assumption that anti-Semitism was an outmoded relic of a barbaric past as it had appeared to be in Russia and Romania. Germany, after all, was one of the advanced states of Western Europe, one in which emancipation and enlightenment had proceeded most rapidly. The necessity for defense, at home and abroad, seemed clearer and more compelling than ever before.

At the same time, the obligation for relief acquired new dimensions. As anti-Semitism passed from one land to another in Central and Eastern Europe the need of the victims of persecution for political support, economic sustenance, and aid in emigration grew steadily more pressing. The Second World War was the final blow; Jews in every part of Europe felt its disastrous impact and their coreligionists in America felt, correspondingly, the heightened urgency for coming to their aid. The growing emphasis upon defensive and relief measures in this decade contributed substantially to the sense of cohesion among the Jews of the United States.

Finally, the development of political Zionism, after 1930, had the same effect. There had been an active, organized Zionist movement in the United States from the end of the nineteenth century onward. But important factors had inhibited its growth. In both the old Eastern European and the old German groups, powerful forces resisted the development of Zionism. The dominant emphasis of the Reform movement among the "German" Jews of the United States had been upon the permanence of settlement in America. The messianic conception had been transmuted into a symbol of general spiritual regeneration unconnected with any physical return to the Holy Land. Among the "Russians," the radical labor element was disposed to view Zionism as but a diversionary tactic that called attention away from the fundamental injustices of society and that confused the masses. For the Orthodox, the return to Zion was a religious rather than a political event, one that would be brought about in proper course through God's will, rather than through the organized action of men.

Resistance from so many sources deprived Zionism, in the early decade of the century, of the opportunity for recruiting a mass membership. The Zionist movement remained quite small, confined to relatively few idealistic and romantic spirits. On occasions it gained the support of others who thought of Palestine as a place of refuge or as a cultural and intellectual center. But down to the 1930's, the conception of a Jewish state was not widely held in the United States.

The situation changed after 1930. The strength of Nazism created the immediate problem of resettling those of its victims who could escape. With immigration to the United States no longer feasible, and with most other countries also closing their gates to newcomers, the only practical place for resettlement, it seemed, was in Palestine. Yet the intransigent attitude of Great Britain, the mandatory power, narrowed the number of immigrants admitted, and threatened soon to cut it off entirely. The resultant dilemma persuaded many Americans that the only means of saving the refugees and, ultimately, the only means of establishing the national home envisaged in the Balfour Declaration was through the creation of an independent political state.

What was more, the shocking failure of emancipation in Germany nurtured an insidious doubt: Would a minority of Jews anywhere in "exile" be able to stave off the anti-Semites? If no settlement could be considered permanently secure, was it not the part of wisdom to safeguard the future in a State of one's own?

All these factors coalesced to transform the predominant attitude into one favorable to political Zionism; and that, increasingly, pushed to the background the older divisive issues.

By the time the Second World War added its own burden of problems, the lines between the German and the East European communities were growing ever less distinct; they had been replaced by a common community, the central concerns of which were defense, relief, and Zionism. Within that community divisions still existed. However, these divisions followed not the old, but new social, economic, and ideological lines.

Since the end of the war in 1945 a third phase had become clear. This period is still in process; indeed, it has only just begun. Its character is therefore of necessity fluid and discernible only in general outline. Yet certain features may already be distinguished with some definiteness.

The institutions inherited from the period of high immigration have either entered upon a decline or have been completely transformed. Since 1945, the volume of immigration has been exceedingly low. The displaced persons of the decade that followed, like the refugees of the 1930's, added an interesting element to the Jewish population, but one too small significantly to affect its long-term development. Consistently the percentage of foreign-born among the American Jews has declined; and the whole complex of social, philanthropic, and economic organizations that sprang from immigration have lost their original reasons for being. Sometimes the institutions themselves have been abandoned by their

membership and have disappeared. Or else, they have been able
to continue either through inertia or through gradual adjustment
of their forms and functions to the changing needs and ideas of
their members.

The pressures of the second period have also abated. The need
for overseas relief continued into the postwar years, reaching its
height in 1948. But this need, though still cheerfully met, is per-
ceptibly on the way toward solution. It is already less important
as a factor in the life of the community than it was five years ago.
Tragically, the largest communities of European Jews have alto-
gether disappeared; and their remnants are no longer as dependent
as they were earlier.

By the same token, the urgency of defense activities has di-
minished. Overt anti-Semitism, for all intents and purposes, disappeared during the war and did not revive thereafter. Instead,
the decade that followed saw a progressive amelioration of the
prejudices from which Jews had earlier suffered. The old patterns
of economic, educational, and social discrimination became ever
less restrictive, as the nation more closely approximated the ideal
of equality of opportunity. The government itself often inter-
ceded on behalf of the minorities, and Jews acquired a greater
sense of security in the preservation of their rights. The tensions
of the preceding decades relaxed; and, although the defense
agencies themselves continued, their work, in the process, took on
a new character. They tended increasingly to occupy themselves
with the general positive problems of improving group relations
and were less often concerned with the narrower questions of
protection against prejudice.

Finally, the whole status of Zionism changed with the emergence
of the state of Israel. Zionism was a practicable program for the
mass of American Jews so long as the Jewish state was not in existence; men could then labor for it without undue concern as to
how it would affect their own role as citizens in the United States.
But, once Israel came into being it posed an unavoidable challenge.
American Jews were then compelled to confront the question of
whether they really believed that a whole Jewish life was possible
only in Israel. An affirmative answer entailed the obligation to
emigrate; and only a handful took that course. (The overwhelm-

ing majority of Zionists now began to understand that they had not been in exile and that the United States was indeed their home. But to accept that conclusion was to raise up a host of other even more troubling questions, concerning the nature of their future ties with Israel and concerning the rationale for their persistence as a group in the United States. In any case, Zionism ceased to be the clearly defined focal point of Jewish organization it had earlier been.

If defense and Zionism, like philanthropy, now ceased to be the dominant preoccupations of American Jews, the Jews nonetheless continued to display a tendency to hold together and to act as a community. The forms of common action persist as does the sense of identification, as a group. Only, that identification now, increasingly, revolves about a religious focus.

That development does not reflect a revival of interest in theology or a restoration of traditional faith. Rather, as with many other ethnic groups in the United States, it represented a turn to religious forms for the satisfaction of complex social needs, earlier otherwise satisfied. The synagogues and temples offered the Jews, as the churches did other Americans, the recognized means by which to organize broad areas of their social life in terms that would assure the continuity of the ethnic group. Given the diversity of sects in the United States no group is peculiar if its separateness is embodied in a religious difference. Given the inclination to form marriages within denominational lines, the oncoming generation can discover a meaningful point of orientation in its religious affiliation. And given the desire for security and stability in the postwar decade, there is a special value to affiliations with traditional roots. It seems likely that these developments will continue to reshape the Jewish community in new and perhaps unexpected ways.

There is a social basis for the changes of the last decade, and that permits at least tentative judgments as to their potential permanence. For the shift of group interests to a religious focus corresponds to a profound transformation of the character of the group itself. The proletariat, once the largest element in the Jewish population, has all but totally disappeared. At the opening of the century a very substantial, and growing, percentage of American Jews were laborers in the "needle" and other trades. But, as the immigrant generation vanished that percentage began to decline. The children of the laborers did not follow their parents into the factories. (Instead, they used the opportunities of American life to enter the professions and to engage in commerce. Down until the 1930's, discrimination and other barriers held back the flow into these occupations. Since 1939 it has proceeded at an accelerating pace.

The definition of the middle class character of the group has involved it in a quest for the kinds of social stability and security that all Americans of that class now seek; and religious identification provides the instruments for attaining those ends. Such identification supplies a source of tradition, a guide against the shocks of a changing world, and a durable standard of behavior. It thus meets the wants of people who, at the same time, are moving from the cities to the suburbs, are attempting to strengthen family ties, and are seeking fresh cultural values and educational goals.

In some sectors of the community there is also an effort to find a speculative foundation for the sense of religious identification, one that will resolve the conflict of tradition and modernity, of faith and science. This effort extends through the Reform, the Orthodox, and the Conservative movements; and it may some day lead to interesting intellectual results. But it has not yet significantly spread from the minority of the intellectuals to the mass of Jews for whom that identification is still primarily the mode of organizing their social life as they move through the third phase of this American experience.

CHAPTER V

The American Negro

IRA DE A. REID

I

A group's conception of itself as a minority arises only after the fact of minority status has been thrust upon it. Any effort to interpret the status of a group so defined without recognition of this fact might well result in an intellectual exercise that promises to yield little more than historical sleight-of-hand. Once this status is achieved, one must recognize that it is maintained not in the splendid isolation of segregation or discrimination, but through partial segregation and partial discrimination, for the survival of the minority and of the power group within a society depends upon the ways in which these communities interact as groups. Beyond this level of operation is another salient fact—the status and the interaction noted in minority group problems in the United States are functions of the dynamics of minority status. What the group does as a minority is done in order to support its feeling of self-regard, to provide meaning for its position and survival, and to develop strategies with which to deal with the problems the status has thrust upon them. It is within this context that I present this discussion of the American Negro.

The minority group status is one of constant uncertainty and ambivalence. No minority group can remain in such a status and deal with the survival issues it must meet. In the group's search for meaning, in its efforts to seek solutions for the problems it faces, in its effort to organize its collective experience, minorities tend to organize movements, to develop leaders, and to develop survival techniques that become important criteria for evaluating their relationship to the total society. The movements that have been organized by the American Negro tend to represent the actions taken when Negroes are confronted by an extrinsic, external environment that is not receptive to them and with which they wish to deal. Looking at this ideal-type minority group within this frame of reference, we are permitted to discover some of the hidden meanings of minority status and to note areas of interaction which are not necessarily unfolded in the usual *recitatifs* of progress or the plaints of second-class citizenship.

Dynamic changes in Negro minority life are singularly impressive when seen in relation to the crises, the movements, and the leadership which spawned them. With crisis upon crisis, the last century has borne the weight of a revolutionary change in the ideology of race adjustment. Leaders, dreamers, and rebels helped to effect this change. Many of them and many of the movements with which they were identified will remain unsung, but all of them were part of a functional leadership and a group expression that directed the goal of the Negro minority from one of isolation and attempted self-sufficiency to integration and the search for a common humanity.

II

Prior to the twentieth century there were four significant social movements that sought to alter the face of Negro-white relations in the United States. Not all of these were movements of the Negro group. In fact, most of them were movements initiated in behalf of the Negro minority rather than by it. The movement for the manumission of slaves, for example, received great impetus as a result of the Battle of Lexington in 1780 when manumission was granted to Negro soldiers and their families because of the former's war efforts. The second major movement, that of efforts to abolish slavery as a social fact in the United States, was essentially a two-part movement. The treble notes were played by the white leaders in the Abolition movement, aided and supported by such "Black Abolitionists" as Frederick Douglass, Prince Hall, Benjamin Banneker, Richard Allen, and Isabella, or Sojourner Truth. The movement was attended by the rise of the Negro Convention movement, and the rise of the Negro press. Two significant phases of this movement took place in Rochester—the first was launching in 1847 of the Abolitionist paper, *The North Star*, by Frederick Douglass, Austin Steward, and Martin R. Delany, a paper dedicated "to the cause of our long oppressed and plundered fellow countrymen." The second was the convening of the National Council of Colored People in July, 1853, a convention attended by one hundred and fourteen very vocal delegates. The mass participation of the Negro people in this movement to abolish slavery was not in this treble clef theme; rather was it heard in the omnibus bass notes of slave revolts, the revolts of Gabriel, Denmark Vesey, and Nat Turner.

Similarly, the movement for colonization of the Negro cannot be classed as one in which Negroes played a positive role. The efforts of the African Colonization Society found no more ready response among the transplanted African peoples than would any contemporary movement to repatriate a group of our foreign-born citizens. President Lincoln's efforts to settle the slavery readjustment pocess in 1862, through encouraging emigration to Haiti and Liberia, found few ready takers. An effort to resettle ex-slaves in some South American country, a plan later limited to the only areas accepting our offer—Panama and the Caribbean island Ile à Vache—did not seem to impress those Negro representatives Lincoln invited to the Capitol to discuss this matter. It was, however, during the Reconstruction movement, that acute period between 1869 and 1901, that the voices of Negroes were heard in concerted pitch within the rising roar of social readjustment. It was during this period of acute conflict, this tragic era, as Claude Bowers has called it, that the American Negro played his most tragic minority role.

The Negro minority movements of the Reconstruction period were both defensive and offensive ones, at once racially separatist and socially integrative. Out of the maelstrom of the period came the infamous Black Codes as well as the election of two Negroes to the United States Senate and of twenty to the House of Representatives. Negroes were members of the executive and legislative branches of many of the state governments in the South. Negro workers were struggling for admittance into the labor union movement while the more modern evil of sharecropping was beginning to infest the agricultural lands. There were efforts to establish Negro businesses, yet the government-initiated Freedmen's Bank failed and with it went the savings of thousands of Negro depositors. During this period many organizations appeared to rebuff, as it were, the resurging wave of white supremacy. There was the founding of Tuskegee Institute, the establishment of the National Association of Colored Men, the launching of the famous Tuskegee Institute Conferences, and the rise of the American Negro Academy with its interest in "arts, science, literature, scholarly works, and the defense of the Negro." The Northern missionary activity was at its zenith in establishing schools and colleges for Negroes, and the lynching of whites and Negroes was reaching a new high. As the nineteenth century moved to a close, Booker T. Washington made his famous Atlanta Cotton States Exposition address in which he drew a blueprint for racial adjustment that immediately gave a new dimension to the Negro's status as a minority group. The dimension was that of a recognized leader or spokesman, recognized without the Negro group if not within it, Booker T. Washington. The dimension was that of an ideological schism within the Negro group, a schism that gave rise to organizations speaking and acting in behalf of political and social rights as well as in behalf of the educated Negro, typed by the group's most outspoken voice, W. E. B. DuBois, as "The Talented Tenth." Not one of the famous protest organizations known to the contemporary United States had arisen at the end of that century. Only two Negroes had reached a stature of eminence during that hundred years—Frederick Douglass in the middle decades and Booker T. Washington in its last twenty years. In terms of movements of the broad sweep, the contributions of the nineteenth century to the present status of the American Negro seem to rest here.

III

It is somewhat ironic that the many serious crises the American Negro has faced during the current century seem to have produced no comprehensive race movement, no significant race leader. More racial riots than the nation has ever known in such a short space of time broke out in Brownsville, Atlanta, Chicago, Washington, Tulsa, Elaine, Springfield, Detroit, and New York. Yet, not an outstanding national leader arose from their ashes. The lynchings of the century, numerous until ten years ago, provided strong arms of propaganda and demands for social action but never sired a special race-leader. Two wars tested democratic truth, but the exigencies of both conflagrations produced neither permanent movements nor new aggressive champions. Finally, the two outstanding movements of this century—the migrations of Negroes from South to North and from farm to factory, and the rise of race-relations-promoting movements—were leaderless. One might well assume that such aspects of human relationships as are reflected in these crises should and would provide recognized leadership and movements for the group's chronic adjustment, names and events that would be remembered because of their significant roles in periods of crisis. That such is not the case reveals the singular nature of Negro minority group adjustment in our racially bifurcated society.

With a few exceptions, the names of persons whose leadership roles have been directed toward the dynamic elimination or amelioration of the problems are without honor and memory within our culture. Our obeisance and homage are rendered to the men and women who made good as individuals, who fought against the odds of being Negro and won acclaim. These persons are essentially of the group politely known as middle-class, professional, commercially enterprising, or artistic, who have made significant contributions in a special field of social activity. Seldom are their names synonymous with racial leadership among the rank and file of the Negro community, save as they appear in the daily or Negro press. In the main, these symbolic leaders pass their usual fretful hours upon the stage of racial fame and then are heard no more. When, a few years ago, a group of racially learned Negro graduate students was asked to identify the names of the twenty persons who between 1915 and 1934 were awarded the Spingarn Medal—an award made annually to a colored person for having reached the highest achievement in his field of activity during a given year—only seven persons were correctly identified by any member of the group. The patent fact seems to be that racial leadership has been identified with individual achievement in spite of the group-limited handicaps rather than with group activity directed toward minority group goals.

However, a more substantial framework within which to identify the American Negro minority group would be provided if one were to identify its leadership with the types of group expressions or group movements that have had a significant effect upon the society's democratic well-being. Two definitions seem essential to this interpretation. Minority group leadership we define as the quality and ability of directing and persuading socially defined groups known as minorities, or the members thereof, toward a specific goal, the possessor of such qualities being followed from free choice, without coercion, and on more or less rational grounds. The term social movement is defined as the collective action of individuals and groups in pursuit of a previously defined goal. The quality of the minority group leader or Messiah is not ascribed to an individual if he or she derives the leadership from office or from an established position as a functionary. However, if this symbolic leadership is represented in a person of the creative type such a one could be identified as leader. Similarly, a mere organizational program for ameliorating or eliminating a social condition does not qualify that program for classification as a social movement. Neither minority group leadership nor minority group movements may be interpreted in terms of such functional sub-aspects as business, education, politics, and the like. Our concern is with the intrinsic racial value that is comprehended by the totality of the Negro minority group situation, however it may be defined by the movement's proponents. What interpretation of the American

Negro's minority group situation does such a theoretical scheme permit?

From the point of view of Negro hopes, aspirations, and activity, the present century is marked by the development of ten significant racial movements. These movements are not classified on the basis of accommodation or protest, nor are they presented as either gradualist or revolutionary; rather are they regarded as socially identifiable operating groups that effected significant changes in the patterns of Negro adjustment in the United States, and did so through the allegiance of relatively large numbers of adherents, with or without a recognized leader. Presented with an eye toward their social chronology, the selected movements follow.

THE TUSKEGEE IDEA

Symbolized by the leadership of Booker T. Washington, this movement perhaps did more to weave the pattern of the material-istic organization of the Negro community than any other. De-signed on the loom of the American success story of "work hard and develop your economic potential," the Idea was persuasive and effective because it caught the Negro community where it was, and through its implementation bade fair to keep it on that plane. The Idea generated a Negro pseudo-economy based on small busi-ness, agricultural enterprise, vocational training, and philanthropy. The Idea opened the doors of functional cooperation and collab-oration between white and colored people, while arresting the consideration of many aspects of freedom and the liberty that democracy should offer. It was significant as a movement because its financial support came largely from persons without the Negro group, because its leadership first received recognition from with-out the group, and because its acceptance by many Negroes was almost a command performance, since they were told that thereby they could at least get one foot in the doorway of democracy. No movement of the century provoked such pervasive internal com-bustion within the Negro community as did the Tuskegee Idea. No leader so captured the imagination of the American people on the race issue as did Booker T. Washington with his separate-as-the-fingers, together-as-the-hand philosophy of minority group ad-justment.

THE NIAGARA MOVEMENT

Not recognized by many persons of the current generation is the movement of half a century ago spearheaded by the "radicals" of the period and symbolized by the leadership of W. E. B. DuBois. This movement that sought to keep alive the dynamic liberalism that was carried on in the anti-slavery campaign, that stood for recognition of all human rights for all men, that fought political discrimination with all of the words and spirit at its command, was the advance agent for the basically democratic minority group crusades of the century. This was the first group to openly consider aggressive action against the racial practices that had developed since Reconstruction. It made possible the development of the National Association for the Advancement of Colored People, and the first real effort of Negroes and whites to end segregation and to work for the enforcement of the Fourteenth and Fifteenth Amendments. Furthermore, the movement and its offspring promoted the idea of human rights at a time when that subject was not regarded as a first thing that should be first considered. The saga of its leader DuBois, alternately fearless and fearful, always the fervent, poetic protagonist, is one of intelligence and passion. It spans the racial vicissitudes of the half-century as does no other man's activity. Known by name to many, in person to few, DuBois stands out as the ideational leader of the movement once regarded as an antithetical idea, but which since has been becoming one with world movements for the liberation of man from his politically manufactured manacles.

THE GREAT MIGRATION

The movement of millions of Negro peoples from South to North and West between 1916 and 1935 permitted or effected changes in Negro group adjustment that have no parallel in United States history. The movement undid many of the evils resulting from (1) the plantation system that survived the Civil War, (2) a somewhat ineffective program of economic reconstruction, and (3) the machinations of political groups, South and North. Ironically, this mass movement had no leader. It needed none. And though the redistribution of Negro and white populations tended to broaden the geographical arena of racial misunderstanding and to widen the arena of racial conflicts, it also provoked rational and political considerations of and action upon the problems involved in the adjustment of relations between white and colored persons in the United States.

THE RACE RELATIONS MOVEMENT

This movement which arose in the South shortly after the First World War, was also a leaderless one. In retrospect, the names of many persons active at its incipient stages come to mind. Yet, no one person can be said to symbolize the movement that was composed of small groups of white and colored persons meeting in cities and hamlets, North and South, discussing ways of preventing outbreaks, or of doing something constructive about the relations between the races. It is a long pull in minority group relations from the first movements with a few "Christian" whites and a quota of "safe" Negroes to the present type of organizations in this field—the municipal and state fair employment and fair education practices commissions, commissions against discrimination, and the like. However, the not-too-fine hand of the movement has been made evident throughout American life, and has even sought to smooth out wrinkles in the racial fabric of South Africa.

THE BACK-TO-AFRICA MOVEMENT

More popularly known as the "Garvey Movement" after its leader, Marcus Garvey, corporately known as the Universal Negro Improvement Association, this mass movement was based upon the idea that since "black" men and women had no chance in the United States they should set up an independent Negro nation in Africa. Developing at a time of world migration, the movement appealed to hundreds of thousands of disillusioned, frustrated colored persons, native and foreign-born. This secular movement is significant because it was based upon race consciousness, a value system in which that which was black or "pure Negro" was best. Garvey in his movement challenged white America and the not-too-mass-conscious Negro movements as they had never been challenged. And despite the fact that the movement failed, that the leader was sent to the Atlanta Federal Penitentiary on a charge of using the mails to defraud, Garvey continued to represent hope to millions of people. A truly charismatic leader, he wrote his followers that if he should die in the penitentiary, they were to look for him "in whirlwind or the storm, look for me all around you, for with God's grace, I shall come and bring with me the countless millions of black slaves who have died in America and the West Indies and the millions in Africa to aid you in the fight for liberty, freedom and life." Garvey did not die in Atlanta, but in London. The UNIA did not survive the errors of its administration, but the "Promised Land" fiction of colonization in Africa, current in the nineteenth century, again found acceptance among the hope-seeking masses of the United States.

The Kingdom of Father Divine

The Divine divinity is included in the status-changing movements of the period because George Baker, Father Divine, happens to be a Negro heading a cult movement of white and colored persons in which any form of racial prejudice is forbidden, which offered food, shelter, peace, and security of its sort to "bewildered and helpless souls" when there was need for them, and which espoused a most forthright and sincere program for racial equality. The movement is significant for its thousands of members because it gave meaning to the individual members and the world, and it raised the status of persons who, in the world of realities, might be considered nobodies. The movement is important because it caught the imagination of non-followers who have introduced into the nation's colloquial vocabulary the expressions—symbols of the movement—"Peace, it is wonderful" and "Thank you, Father." Because Father Divine is brown of skin; because so many of his followers are persons of color; because he can purchase so many hotels with thousands of dollars in currency; because so many people saw a causal relation in the fact that (1) a judge died three days after sentencing Father Divine to jail, (2) Will Rogers' plane crashed a short time after he had made some unfavorable remark about the Father in a radio broadcast, and (3) Huey Long was assassinated a few days after refusing to see one of Divine's Peace Mission delegations; because in God's sight there is no difference in color, and persons may not use the words "white," "black," or

"Negro" in the kingdoms; because of all this, the changing minority status of the American Negro must be designated, in part at least, as occurring in the period which follows the dates appearing in any publications of the movement—ADFD, *Anno Domini Father Divine*.

THE NEGRO WOMAN MOVEMENT

At the turn of the century there was established the National Association of Colored Women. Some twenty years ago, the late Mary McLeod Bethune, affectionately known to many of her colleagues in racial and national affairs as "Mother Messiah," organized the National Council of Negro Women, an organization said to represent a membership of eight hundred thousand women. The creation of the organization was but a symbol of the dynamic change that had been made in the quantity and quality of social action exerted by colored women during the century. Women's clubs, formerly sewing, knitting, and embroidery circles, or literary organizations interested in doing charitable deeds for the poor, became agencies of social pressure, active in politics, pressing for education, attacking the problems of lynching, riots, and race relations, and working for social welfare for all peoples. In the early part of the century the women's clubs were represented by the "intellectual," the "Lady Bountiful" types of women who lived chiefly in the North. The Mary McLeod Bethune era introduced the programs of action, widened the quantity and the character of membership, and above all, reduced the class emphasis in Negro woman leadership. No one person incorporated so many of the minority group symbols as did this "large, black, full-bosomed and strong-limbed" plantation-born, mission-school-trained, Mary Bethune. No leaven in the changing status of the Negro minority was more powerful than that which came from the widely dispersed membership which she headed.

THE MARCH-ON-WASHINGTON MOVEMENT

This was a concentrated mass protest action-program directed against the policies of the Federal Government during the so-called "defense period" preceding the Second World War. Spearheaded by A. Philip Randolph, president of the Brotherhood of Sleeping

Car Porters, who for more than thirty years has been an inde-
fatigable worker for the trade union organization of Negro workers, the movement was significant because (1) it revealed at once
the weaknesses of existing minority groups' movements that did
not have a mass base; (2) it showed that social classes within the
Negro group could be combined in effective social action; (3)
it succeeded in bringing into being during the war emergency the
famous Presidential Order 8802 which forbade contractors holding government contracts to discriminate against workers because
of their race, creed, color, or national origin; and (4) it organized
support for the movement which has resulted in agitation for and
establishment of commissions on fair employment practices.
Though of shorter life span than any other movement included in
this analysis, the March-on-Washington activity must be regarded
as an effective demonstration of action and leadership, at work in a
crisis situation, that led to long-range changes in the character of
the race system in this country.

THE PEOPLE-OF-THE-WORLD-MOVEMENT

The last quarter of a century has witnessed the development of
a new dimension in the American Negro's minority group status—
its international significance. Since the First World War there
have been many manifestations of this international-mindedness.
Yesterday's organizational movement of the Pan-African Con-
gresses initiated by DuBois bears almost no resemblance to the
current discussions and programs that seek to bring about more
substantial changes in the relationships of darker peoples with their
peers and masters throughout the world. Movements in behalf
of the peoples and free movements of Africa—East, West, and
South—movements in behalf of the populations of the Caribbean,
and common cause with the brown peoples of the Asias reflect
this interest. The followers of this generalized and amorphous
movement cannot be numbered, nor can the movement be dis-
missed as unimportant. There are many reasons for believing that
the movement promised to be the dynamic movement of the century. It was able to exact more intense loyalties than many of the
more provincial race movements. It was able to cause many people
to reason that there must be something rather basic in the idea that

a new order of human relations in industrial society is not built
with the dulled tools of a handicraft period. They reason that
there should be no race system in the new society. Among Negro
people of the United States there may be disagreement over and
rejection of the *means* such a movement would employ; they may
be uncertain as to whether they should choose the road of a Ralph
Bunche or that of a Paul Robeson; but there is a practical unanimity in the desirability of ends that promise the end of race as a
symbol and of a system of inequality and exploitation.

THE LEGAL CRUSADE

The final movement in this saga of the Negro's changing status
as a minority group is the story of the group's changing status
and changing self-conception arising out of a series of decisions by
the United States Supreme Court that have defined and supported
the group's quest for civil rights. Initiated by the National Association for the Advancement of Colored People's legal staff, the
crusade has for more than thirty years waged war against those
situations which the Negro group has defined as entrenched discrimination and segregation. Regarded not so many years ago as
one of the necessary but futile gestures in the democratic process,
the legal victories have perhaps done more than any other movement in reshaping the status of the American Negro minority. Not
only is the formula of second-class citizenship removed from the
approved practices of government in operation; not only has the
method of political participation been altered in at least fifteen of
our several states; but, in addition, the decisions have necessitated a
complete revision of Negro life itself. A group that has been somewhat ambivalent about the merits of separation and segregation
because many of them have profited therefrom is now forced to
come out from its protective racialism and face the competition
and the realities of what promises to be full citizenship. This,
perhaps, is the most serious status-altering device the American
Negro has ever had to face. As a result, this group stands on the
brink of one of the most significant group readjustments of modern times—peaceful reformation of its inner meaning. In the
language of the Supreme Court when it handed down its decree
that there may be no discrimination in public parks or on public

beaches where governmental funds are used, "the motion to affirm is granted and the judgment is affirmed."

From the points of view of social history and social action the above movements seem to be the outstanding ones through which to view the changing status of the American Negro minority as that minority has met the situations determining its status. And though history has a strange way of idolizing and idealizing the select, the propagandized, and the socially approved crisis, movement, or leader, it also reveals how easily one may err in evaluating the directions men take in their search for peace, equality, security, and that undefinable—something more.

CHAPTER VI

The Japanese American[1]

DOROTHY SWAINE THOMAS

I. PREWAR

Japanese immigrants began coming to the United States during the 1880's, and most of them settled in the Pacific Coast states. At their prewar maximum, they and their American-born descendants represented less than 3 per cent of the total population in California, the state where the vast majority settled and established families. From 1891 (the first year for which official statistics are available) through 1924, when Oriental exclusion was incorporated in our immigration law, there were only six years when as many as 10,000 Japanese aliens entered American ports directly from Japan, and no single year when the number reached 15,000. Of those who came to these shores, many returned to the homeland, and from 1908, when the Gentlemen's Agreement became effective, through 1924, the net balance of aliens entering over those departing represented an average increment of less than 1,000 per year; from 1925 to the outbreak of the Second World War, there was a consistent net loss, averaging almost 2,000 per year. In 1940, the Japanese minority in the continental United States numbered only 127,000:

90 per cent of them lived on the Pacific Coast and 74 per cent in California. By this time, the American-born *Nisei* outstripped the foreign-born *Issei* in the ratio of two to one. Half of the Nisei were under 17 years of age; and one in three of those over 25 years of age had been educated wholly or in part in Japan. Returning to America—for the most part during the 1930's—this culturally marginal subgroup of the American-born was known as *Kibei*.[2]

In spite of their small numbers and low density, Japanese Americans were, from the earliest days, a politically unpopular minority, and the object of discriminatory laws and practices, especially in California.

In accordance with various judicial interpretations of our Naturalization Act of 1790, and of its subsequent amendments and revisions, Japanese aliens were racially ineligible for American citizenship. For a short period—between 1935 and 1937—Congress removed the barriers to naturalization for Japanese aliens who had served in our armed forces during the First World War—but these were numerically unimportant exceptions to the rule that persons of Japanese "blood" born on alien soil were ineligible for naturalization, however long and under whatever conditions they had resided in this country. Nisei and Kibei, however, by virtue of birth on American soil, held the American citizenship that Issei could not obtain through naturalization.

"Ineligibility for citizenship" provided the legal basis for discriminatory procedures, especially at both state and national levels. To Issei it became a constant reminder of the racial intolerance of the majority group, and a constant threat to their security. The threat was actualized in the land laws passed in California between 1913 and 1923 (and later imitated elsewhere in the West), affirming rights of aliens who could become naturalized citizens to possess land, and denying these same rights to aliens "ineligible for citizenship." And "ineligibility for citizenship" was the basis for Oriental exclusion in the Immigration Act of 1924. The Issei nevertheless obtained a pivotal place in the Western farm economy, especially in California, where they accommodated themselves to the requirements of a mobile, seasonal labor force. Organizing first in gangs of single men, they took over much of the onerous stoop labor required in intensive vegetable and berry cultivation, and, in the beginning, they undercut on wages. Marrying and founding families, many moved from the ranks of labor to tenancy and even to ownership, protected in numerous instances by the citizenship status of their children or assisted in collusive evasion by Caucasian ranchers. They developed small holdings as family enterprises; they cleared and drained and brought raw land under cultivation; they specialized and intensified even beyond prevailing practices; they paid high rents and they accepted substandard housing. With the expenditure of relatively little capital, this small minority was, by 1941, producing 30–35 per cent of California's total truck crops.

Most of the early Issei urban enterprises served merely to meet the needs of the expanding ethnic group. When they attempted to broaden the base for a larger public, they met serious opposition from organized labor, especially in San Francisco, where their competition in laundries, in restaurants, and in many other activities, was effectively restrained through boycotts, and it was almost impossible for them to penetrate the ranks of skilled labor. In Seattle, however, Japanese-operated restaurants held their own, and hotels and grocery stores expanded far beyond the confines of the ethnic communities. Their most notable success was in Los Angeles, particularly in enterprises concerned with the marketing of agricultural produce, where, just before the outbreak of the Second World War, they are said to have handled 60 per cent of the volume of wholesale business and they almost monopolized fruit-and-vegetable concessions in retail shops and markets. Their success in these fields was due, in large measure, to intensive application of labor, to meticulous attention to detail, and to constant care in eliminating wastage. To these ends, most entrepreneurs used family help to the maximum, required long hours of their other low-paid, unorganized helpers, and themselves gave unstintedly of their time.

The Japanese placed a high cultural value upon education, and although the Issei's ambivalence and insecurity led them to promote practices that might make their children acceptable either in Japan or in the United States, the Nisei utilized American educational facilities to the fullest possible extent, with far-reaching consequences in the development of American habits and attitudes and in thus promoting rapid assimilation. By every available index,

American-educated children of Japanese parentage were more thoroughly schooled than even the notably well-educated general population (of comparable age and sex distribution) on the Pacific Coast. In grade level attained, they greatly surpassed any other identifiable minority, and approximated that of native whites. Compared with other population groups, Nisei children started school earlier and remained in school longer through the adolescent period; they completed full curricula more often; they obtained better grades and ratings from teachers; and they received a quite disproportionate number of scholastic honors. Moreover, as tested in California schools during the 1930's, their vocational aptitudes were assessed by E. K. Strong and his associates as "remarkably similar" to those of the whites and led them to conclude that "insofar as interests determine one's life career . . . Japanese and whites should enter occupations in practically the same proportions." [3]

The return of the Kibei tended to aggravate cultural diversity within many families, for it was usually only one or two of several siblings who had been sent to Japan.[4] Most Issei fathers had grown up in the Japan of the late nineteenth and the very early twentieth century, and the residence in Japan of Issei mothers had terminated before America's entrance into the First World War. The Kibei child in most families had completed his education in the aggressively nationalistic Japan of the 1930's, while the Nisei children had had no direct contact with the land of their parents. Conflict, which might have occurred normally between the generations and among siblings, was intensified by extreme environmental and temporal contrasts, and the situation was further complicated when culture conflict became tinged with political implications. Behavior and attitudes of Issei and particularly of Kibei, which had been censured as "Japanesy" by the Nisei, even when their own family relationships were characterized by warmth and mutual tolerance, were widely condemned as "pro-Japan" during the late 1930's and particularly after 1940. Generational and sibling cleavages were sharpened by real or imagined divergent national loyalties.

The economic position of American-born Japanese contrasted unfavorably, at the outbreak of war, both with that of their peers in the majority group and with that of the parental generation. The former is indicated in Table I (adapted from *The Salvage*),

TABLE I. PERCENTAGE DISTRIBUTIONS BY OCCUPATION OF EMPLOYED LABOR FORCE 14 YEARS OF AGE AND OLDER; AND DIFFERENCES BETWEEN THESE DISTRIBUTIONS, BY SEX, AMERICAN-BORN JAPANESE AND TOTAL POPULATION, CALIFORNIA, 1940

	Male			Female		
	(1)	(2)		(3)	(4)	
		Total			Total	
	American-	Population		American-	Population	
	Born	Standard-		Born	Standard-	
	Japanese,	ized to Age		Japanese,	ized to Age	
Occupation	Aged 14+	of Japanese	(1) − (2)	Aged 14+	of Japanese	(3) − (4)
Professional	4.4	7.1	− 2.7	5.1	12.2	− 7.1
Proprietors, etc.	14.3	7.2	+ 7.1	4.1	2.3	+ 1.8
Clerical and sales	31.9	21.8	+10.1	30.1	44.3	−14.2
Craftsmen	4.3	15.8	−11.5	0.7	0.6	+ 0.1
Operatives	16.4	24.1	− 7.7	9.2	11.6	− 2.4
Service (except private household)	5.4	13.0	− 7.6	12.0	15.2	− 3.2
Private household workers	6.0	0.5	+ 5.5	37.8	13.2	+24.6
Laborers	17.3	10.5	+ 6.8	1.0	0.6	+ 0.4
Total	100.0	100.0	+29.5	100.0	100.0	+26.9
			−29.5			−26.9

Source: Computed from data in U.S. Census of Population, 1940, as used in *The Salvage*, Table 14.

Distributions of the general population were standardized, separately for each sex, to the age distributions of American-born Japanese.

where nonagricultural occupational distributions of American-born Japanese in California, as of 1940, are compared with age-standardized distributions of the general population; the magnitude of the disparity is measured by subtracting each Japanese distribution from its counterpart in the general population and summing the positive and the negative deviations. Had the minority-group distributions deviated only slightly from those of the general population, these sums would have approached zero; had they been completely dissimilar, the sums would have equaled 100 per cent. The observed sums of 30 and 27 per cent, respectively, for the two sexes, are indicative of a considerable degree of dissimilarity, with negative deviations heavily weighted by the professional categories for both sexes and by skilled laborers among males, and clerical and sales personnel among females. Correspondingly, the positive deviations reflect Japanese concentrations on the lowest rungs of the occupational ladder, that is, domestic service for both sexes and unskilled labor for males. Compared with the general population there was also a disproportionate concentration at the clerical-sales level and, to a lesser degree, at the proprietor-managerial level, among Japanese males. Compared with the parental generation, however, relatively few of the American-born had attained independent status as entrepreneurs; and, among the white-collar classes, as can be shown with reference to data collected by the War Relocation Authority, the vast majority still held positions within the ethnic group.

Of Nisei working in trade and nondomestic service enterprises (and later evacuated to relocation projects), 9 out of every 10 of those who came from San Francisco, 4 out of 5 of those from Los Angeles, and 3 out of 4 of those from Seattle held employee status. Although failure to attain independent status was, to some extent, attributable to their youth,[5] Nisei were generally reluctant to take over responsibility for the family enterprises which their fathers had founded. In many cases this would have meant assumption of an intolerable personal burden and perpetuation of a way of life incompatible with American standards. Their economic goal was, rather, to break into the ranks of majority-group activities from which their parents had been excluded. Up to the time of evacuation, but few of them had succeeded in reaching this goal. Close to half of the Nisei employees in trade and service enterprises in San Francisco and over half of those in Los Angeles were in a single type of firm: Oriental-art-goods stores in the former, fruit-and-vegetable markets in the latter. Not even one in ten Nisei employees in trade and nondomestic service was working for a "Caucasian" firm in either San Francisco or Los Angeles, and only two in every ten were so employed in Seattle. There was an occasional opening for a Nisei typist or bookkeeper or mail-order-house salesman, but there were few opportunities for positions requiring face-to-face contact with the general public. Almost all of the doctors, dentists, lawyers, and optometrists served the needs of other Japanese and only rarely had one succeeded in obtaining white clientele or connections with Caucasian-operated institutions, either public or private. Journalists worked for vernacular newspapers. Engineers, accountants, teachers, and social workers found it almost impossible to practice their skills in the wider community. Some technicians, e.g., biochemists and dieticians, obtained positions for which they had been trained, and there was little discrimination against nurses. Civil service, state and federal, offered opportunities to a few white-collar workers. But in the main, most Nisei were, at the outbreak of war, back where their parents had started.

II. THE WAR PERIOD

When the sudden attack on Pearl Harbor precipitated war between the United States and the Axis powers, Japanese, German, and Italian nationals were, alike, declared to be "alien enemies." Their traveling was restricted, their bank accounts were frozen, and their business enterprises were closed. Numbers were apprehended, on suspicion, and held in detention by the F.B.I. or interned. It was announced that all alien enemies might be excluded from military zones.

Because large numbers of German and Italian immigrants had become naturalized, the incidence of the application of these early restrictions was greatest in the Japanese immigrant communities, and, for Issei, the dormant threat to their security of "ineligibility for citizenship" was again revived. Furthermore, there were disturbing indications that the status of the American-born as descendants of the Japanese enemy might take precedence over their status as American citizens. Thus, restrictions on travel referred to "Japanese individuals" and were applied indiscriminately to alien enemies and to American citizens of Japanese ancestry. In some instances, similar interpretations were made in respect to assets. Citizens as well as aliens were stopped on the highways, summarily arrested, and held for questioning.

By the end of the second week of the war a number of the restrictions on alien enemies had been relaxed, and many of the misunderstandings regarding American citizens of Japanese ancestry seemed to have been cleared up. Federal and local officials, educators, clergymen, other prominent citizens, and most of the West Coast newspapers pleaded for tolerance, for the protection of "loyal Japanese" and of "loyal alien enemies" generally, and they emphasized the citizenship rights of the American-born, their record of service in the armed forces, their participation in civilian defense.

By the end of January 1942, our serious reverses in the Pacific area made the West Coast seem increasingly vulnerable to attack or possible invasion. Reports (later shown to have no basis in fact) that Japanese residents had formed a fifth column in Hawaii, given aid and comfort to the enemy, and sabotaged the American defense of Pearl Harbor, were widely circulated. Fears of similar activities among Japanese Americans on the West Coast began to find frequent public expression and crystallized as demands for evacuation and internment. Public fears, organized pressures, further reverses in the Pacific, and anticipated need for vigorous defense of the West Coast finally resulted in national sanction of a regionally evolved plan for total evacuation of the Japanese minority. On February 19, President Roosevelt signed Executive Order 9066 authorizing delimitation of Military Areas "from which any or all persons [might] be excluded." The Commanding General of the Western Defense Command, John L. DeWitt, who was made responsible for implementing the executive order, had already recommended "evacuation of Japanese and *other subversive persons* from the Pacific Coast," [italics supplied] and had specified that "the word 'Japanese' included alien Japanese and American citizens of Japanese ancestry." In later proclamations and directives, General DeWitt referred to the American-born group, euphemistically, as "American-born persons of Japanese lineage," or as "nonalien persons of Japanese ancestry," and in the *Final Report* of the Western Defense Command "Nisei" was defined as "any person of Japanese ancestry not born in Japan," while the meaning of "Japanese ancestry" was clarified to cover "any person who has a Japanese ancestor, regardless of degree." [6]

Verbal disregard for and devaluation of the American citizenship of American-born Japanese had its counterpart in the actions initiated and carried through by the Western Defense Command. On March 2, General DeWitt designated the western third of Washington and Oregon, the western half of California, and the southern quarter of Arizona as "Military Area No. 1," and on the following day announced that a gradual program of exclusion from the area would be applied to the following four classes, in order: Japanese aliens, American-born persons of Japanese lineage, German aliens, and Italian aliens. No mass action was ever taken against Germans and Italians.

The Western Defense Command announced that it planned to clear Military Area No. 1 of all "potential enemies." Deadlines had to be met, but evacuation was to be accomplished voluntarily by the persons or groups covered by successive exclusion orders, and they were to have free choice of destination outside the exclusion areas. By the middle of March, however, it became apparent that voluntary evacuation was not workable. Hostility developed in the eastern counties of California and in the intermountain states, to which a few thousand evacuees had moved. As explained in the Command's *Final Report:*

> This group, considered too dangerous to remain on the West Coast was similarly regarded by state and local authorities, and by the population of the interior. The evacuees were not welcome. Incidents developed with increasing intensity.[7]

Plans for voluntary evacuation and free selection of destinations were scrapped in favor of controlled mass evacuation and detention. To implement this procedure, a public proclamation, issued on March 27, forbade change of residence by persons of Japanese ancestry who were living in Military Area No. 1. On June 2 a similar regulation was issued, covering the eastern half of California —an area which was until then called the "free zone" and was the officially sanctioned destination of about half of all those who had been able to accomplish voluntary evacuation. By August 8, controlled evacuation of the whole of California, and of those parts of Washington, Oregon, and Arizona that lay within Military Area No. 1, had been completed in a series of moves, each move being covered by a specific exclusion order, and announced in posters displayed prominently throughout the area concerned (exemplified in the order for San Diego, shown in Figure 1). Approximately 90,000 persons entered assembly centers, which had been hastily constructed by the Army on nearby race tracks and fair grounds for a "transitory phase" of detention, preliminary to another controlled mass migration. This "transitory phase" lasted from a few weeks to six or seven months. It was followed by a

WESTERN DEFENSE COMMAND AND FOURTH ARMY
WARTIME CIVIL CONTROL ADMINISTRATION
Presidio of San Francisco, California

April 1, 1942

INSTRUCTIONS
TO ALL PERSONS OF
JAPANESE
ANCESTRY
Living in the Following Area:

All of San Diego County, California, south of a line extending in an easterly direction from the mouth of the San Dieguito River (northwest of Del Mar), along the north side of the San Dieguito River, Lake Hodges, and the San Pasqual River to the bridge over the San Pasqual River at or near San Pasqual; thence easterly along the southerly line of California State Highway No. 78 through Ramona and Julian to the eastern boundary line of San Diego County.

All Japanese persons, both alien and non-alien, will be evacuated from the above designated area by 12:00 o'clock noon Wednesday, April 8, 1942.

No Japanese person will be permitted to enter or leave the above described area after 8:00 a. m., Thursday, April 2, 1942, without obtaining special permission from the Provost Marshal at the Civil Control Station located at:

1919 India Street
San Diego, California

The Civil Control Station is equipped to assist the Japanese population affected by this evacuation in the following ways:

1. Give advice and instructions on the evacuation.

2. Provide services with respect to the management, leasing, sale, storage or other disposition of most kinds of property including: real estate, business and professional equipment, buildings, household goods, boats, automobiles, livestock, etc.

3. Provide temporary residence elsewhere for all Japanese in family groups.

4. Transport persons and a limited amount of clothing and equipment to their new residence, as specified below.

The Following Instructions Must Be Observed:

1. A responsible member of each family, preferably the head of the family, or the person in whose name most of the property is held, and each individual living alone, will report to the Civil Control Station to receive further instructions. This must be done between 8:00 a. m. and 5:00 p. m., Thursday, April 2, 1942, or between 8:00 a. m. and 5:00 p. m., Friday, April 3, 1942.

2. Evacuees must carry with them on departure for the Reception Center, the following property:

(a) Bedding and linens (no mattress) for each member of the family;
(b) Toilet articles for each member of the family;
(c) Extra clothing for each member of the family;
(d) Sufficient knives, forks, spoons, plates, bowls and cups for each member of the family;
(e) Essential personal effects for each member of the family.

All items carried will be securely packaged, tied and plainly marked with the name of the owner and numbered in accordance with instructions received at the Civil Control Station.

The size and number of packages is limited to that which can be carried by the individual or family group.

No contraband items as described in paragraph 6, Public Proclamation No. 3, Headquarters Western Defense Command and Fourth Army, dated March 24, 1942, will be carried.

3. The United States Government through its agencies will provide for the storage at the sole risk of the owner of the more substantial household items, such as iceboxes, washing machines, pianos and other heavy furniture. Cooking utensils and other small items will be accepted if crated, packed and plainly marked with the name and address of the owner. Only one name and address will be used by a given family.

4. Each family, and individual living alone, will be furnished transportation to the Reception Center. Private means of transportation will not be utilized. All instructions pertaining to the movement will be obtained at the Civil Control Station.

Go to the Civil Control Station at 1919 India Street, San Diego, California, between 8:00 a. m. and 5:00 p. m., Thursday, April 2, 1942, or between 8:00 a. m. and 5:00 p. m., Friday, April 3, 1942, to receive further instructions.

J. L. DeWITT
Lieutenant General, U. S. Army
Commanding

SEE CIVILIAN EXCLUSION ORDER NO. 4

FIG. 1.

further controlled movement to more permanent camps, called "relocation projects," and administered by a newly formed civilian agency, the War Relocation Authority (W.R.A.). By November 1942, this phase, in turn, was completed when 20,000 evacuees were moved directly from their homes to join the 90,000 who had been confined in assembly centers.

The swiftness with which evacuation was accomplished rendered plans for the protection of evacuee property ineffective. Governmental responsibility was divided between the Farm Security Administration and the Federal Reserve Bank. The aims of the former were to insure continuation of farm production for the war effort and to protect the evacuated farmer from unfair and inequitable transfer. The two aims were frequently incompatible, and, under the circumstances, the first took precedence over the second. The Bank, which had been given responsibility for safeguarding nonagricultural property, undertook a policy of encouraging liquidation, accepted property for storage only "at the sole risk" of the owner, provided no insurance, and disclaimed liability "for any act or omission in connection with [the property's] disposition." Under these conditions, virtually all evacuees suffered heavy losses of tangible assets, and for the many engaged in activities and enterprises which could not be transferred or sold, losses incurred through abandonment of intangible assets were even greater.

Evacuation was a policy proposed by the Western Defense Command, accepted by the War Department, and sanctioned by the President of the United States. Detention of the whole of the West-Coast racial minority in war-duration concentration camps was a policy proposed by no responsible agency, nor was any attempt made to justify it, officially, as a matter of "military necessity"—the basis on which the Command had attempted to justify total evacuation. Detention seemed, at the time, a way out of the dilemma posed by total evacuation, when most of the persons ordered to evacuate were physically, emotionally, economically, culturally, and demographically incapable of finding jobs and homes in other areas, and when the few thousand who had managed to accomplish voluntary evacuation were being met by hostility or suspicion in the receiving areas. Once detention became a reality, however, it ceased to be viewed as a "transitory phase" between evacuation and resettlement, and the W.R.A. program was soon perverted from resettling displaced people to planning a way of life for them within the confines of barbed wire.

In spite of physical hardships, the evacuees were, in the beginning, almost uniformly cooperative, and seemed to share the belief prevalent among W.R.A. officials and employees that a "good life" could be built up in these isolated, war-duration communities. But, before many weeks passed, anti-administration and intergroup hostilities flared into the open. Faith in the good intentions of the administration declined when procurement difficulties arose and shortages of food, of hospital supplies, and of other essentials developed; when promises of producers' cooperatives, under which cash advances on profits were to be distributed to the participating evacuees, were abandoned in favor of what Milton Eisenhower, who was then Director of W.R.A., denounced as "miserably low" [8] remuneration of $12, $16, and $19 per month for jobs ranging from farm labor, cooking, and dishwashing to those of teacher, attorney, and doctor; when payment of even these wages was delayed; when, during the prolonged period of nonpayment, timekeeping systems were introduced by efficiency experts; and when a plan for limited self-government was imposed, which, while enfranchising Issei, made them ineligible for officeholding.

Regional and generational fissures, temporarily closed during the stress of evacuation, were reopened. Rumors of F.B.I. inquiries and arrests aroused suspicions that there were "informers" among fellow evacuees, and cooperation with the administration was branded as "collaboration." Every faction found its convenient scapegoat. Suspected informers were ostracized, threatened, and even beaten by their fellow evacuees. Revolt against the administration took the form of major strikes or minor work-stoppages during the fall of 1942, and in two projects, Poston and Manzanar, revolt assumed the proportions of riots, and was met with force by the administration.

Meantime, the War Relocation Authority was pressing the Justice and War Departments for sanction to reinstitute the program its name implied. By the end of July 1942, a cautious program of highly selective resettlement had been approved, and through cooperation of the Friends Service Committee, had achieved a considerable degree of success against great odds, in relocating students in eastern and midwestern colleges and universities. But for other classes the procedures in obtaining "leave clearance" for release from detention were so unwieldly that only a handful of evacuees had been relocated by the end of 1942. Among the necessary prerequisites to clearance were formal investigations of "loyalty," detailed reports of behavior and attitudes in relocation projects, unequivocal evidence of a valid job offer and of provision for care of dependents remaining in camp, evidence of acceptability in the proposed community of destination, and, for a time, even investigations of each prospective employer.

Determined to liberalize relocation policy, W.R.A. officials agreed to, and indeed promoted, a plan for obtaining mass clearance, following a decision of the War Department to reopen the Army to loyal Japanese-American volunteers. In accordance with this plan, representatives of the War Department were to "process" male citizens, while W.R.A. employees would "process" the remainder of the adult population. In both cases, processing involved registration and the execution of a lengthy questionnaire, including, among some thirty items, two thought to bear directly on "loyalty." For male citizens, the first of these was:

> Are you willing to serve in the armed forces of the United States on combat duty, wherever ordered?

and the second, asked of aliens also:

> Will you swear unqualified allegiance to the United States of America and faithfully defend the United States from any or all attack by foreign or domestic forces, and forswear any form of allegiance or obedience to the Japanese emperor, or any other foreign government, power, or organization?

The impropriety of asking aliens who were ineligible to American citizenship to forswear allegiance to the country in which they held citizenship was recognized belatedly. In most projects aliens were permitted to substitute an oath that they would "abide by the laws of the United States" and "take no action which would in any way interfere with the war effort of the United States." But American citizens, the bulk of whom were Nisei who had had no direct contact with Japan, were still required to forswear allegiance to the Japanese emperor.

Registration was postulated on the assumption that evacuees would define eligibility to serve in the armed service or to leave camps for the freedom of the "outside world" as just rewards for loyalty. Contrary to expectation, an appreciable proportion of the evacuees defined these situations as penalties rather than as rewards. A strong protest movement developed among some Nisei and many Kibei, who, having had so many of their rights as citizens abrogated through evacuation and detention, questioned the justice of the restoration of the single right of serving in the armed forces. Numbers of Issei, having lost most of their other possessions, used every means to hold their families intact, and to prevent the possible induction of their sons. Others, having acceded to a forced migration from home to camp, were now determined to avoid a further move to an outside world that they had many reasons to believe would continue to regard them with hostility.

Doubt, fear, and anger accompanied registration in all relocation projects, and these reactions were aggravated by inadequate preparation of the teams conducting registration; by sudden, unexplained, or incompletely understood changes in administrative procedures and definitions; and in one of the largest camps, Tule Lake, by the use of force. In all projects except Tule Lake the average proportion of the adult population refusing to register or registering as "disloyal," was 10 per cent, but in Tule Lake the unregistered and the verbally disloyal, together, comprised 42 per cent of all persons 17 years of age or older. The persistence of a collective movement of noncooperation at Tule Lake was widely publicized and its residents were stigmatized, in the press and on the radio, as politically disloyal. In July 1943, the Senate passed a resolution asking W.R.A. to segregate in relocation centers persons of Japanese ancestry whose loyalty to the United States was "questionable" or who were known to be "disloyal." W.R.A. yielded and designated Tule Lake as a segregation center in which evacuees whose loyalties were thought to lie with Japan would be confined for the duration of the war.

During the late summer Tule Lake was transformed, physically, from a relocation project to a segregation center. A double "man-

proof" fence, eight feet high, was constructed around the whole
area; the external guard was increased from a couple of hundred
soldiers to full battalion strength; and a half dozen tanks, obsolete
but impressive, were lined up in full view of the residents. The
"loyal" were moved out of Tule Lake to other camps, and the
"disloyal" were moved from these camps to the segregation center.

The conflicts and tensions in Tule Lake after segregation and the
course of interaction between "disloyal" and "loyal," between
groups of evacuees and administrative agencies, and among the
various agencies themselves, are traced in the Thomas-Nishimoto
volume, *The Spoilage*. There was almost immediate revolt, led
by disaffected transferees; an outbreak of violence, following a
labor dispute; and two serious accidents. There was also administrative suppression, involving the importation of "loyal" har-
vesters from other projects as strikebreakers, the institution of
martial law for two months, and the establishment of a "stockade"
in which alleged agitators were confined for periods up to eight
months "without the filing of charges or the granting of a hearing
or trial of any kind." By the spring of 1944 an underground pressure group, in which Kibei were prominently represented, had
come out into the open. In July 1944, the Nationality Act of
1940 was amended to permit the renunciation of citizenship during
wartime by American citizens on American soil, and renunciation
then became the keynote of the campaign of the Kibei-dominated
pressure group.

Two administrative decisions, announced simultaneously on December 17, 1944, further confused the issues. These were (1)
recision of orders by the Western Defense Command excluding
Japanse Americans from the West Coast, and (2) announcement
by the War Relocation Authority that all projects under their
supervision would be liquidated within a year. These decisions,
taken together, imperiled the security of the "disloyal" who believed that they had attained a war-duration refuge in Tule Lake.
For all segregants forced resettlement, and, for the young men of
draft age induction into the armed forces, loomed as disturbingly
high probabilities. By March 1945, seven out of every ten citizens in Tule Lake old enough to be eligible to renounce their

American citizenship had done so, and in so doing had, it was believed, afforded "protection" from forced resettlement to over 3,000 families.

From the standpoint of 1946, and perhaps also in the long run, this is what the authors of the California studies considered "the spoilage." On August 26, 1949, however, the legal basis for the restitution of status for those citizens who became "aliens ineligible for citizenship" in the land of their birth was established through a decision in the United States Court of Appeals for the Ninth Circuit, conforming to a lower court decision which held that

> the benefits of citizenship can be renounced or waived only as a result of free and intelligent choice. Since the purported renunciation . . . was not as a result of . . . free and intelligent choice but rather because of mental fear, intimidation, and coercions depriving them of the free exercise of their will, said purported renunciations are void and of no force or effect.[9]

Evacuation and detention aggravated culture conflict within the already culturally divided Japanese-American population group, and forced dissident elements to redefine their status in America, or to have it defined for them. As described above, some revolted, and many were led toward verbal disloyalty and renunciation of American citizenship. Together, these classes and their dependents represented about one in six of the evacuees in War Relocation projects.

Almost half of the evacuees took the way of least resistance, and simply sat out the war years, behind barbed wire, in the camps provided by the government of the United States. There they lived on what were essentially culture-islands until, with recision of exclusion orders and forced closure of camps, they faced the necessity of evacuation-in-reverse.

More than one in three of the total deliberately chose the difficult path of resettlement in the Middle West or East while the war was still in progress. In so doing they embarked upon a life that, they had been assured, would not be without hardships but that would involve "the same hardships . . . being experienced by other American families." [10] At the same time, they knowingly accepted the special risks and uncertainties to be incurred because of their close physical resemblance to the Japanese enemy. Many of them served with great distinction in the armed forces; others were active in war industries and agencies. Numbers of them moved into the ranks of skilled labor, and into clerical, sales, and professional occupations. Some became disorganized and failed to make adequate vocational, personal, or social adjustments. But, whether narrowly defined as "successes" or as "failures," these were what the authors of the California studies considered to be "the salvage" of the war, to the extent that resettlement broke their isolation, promoted their acceptance by the majority group, and integrated their activities into those of the larger American community.

The salvage was highly selective. Seven out of every ten of the persons involved in the successive waves of outmigration from camps were young people between the ages of 15 and 34. More significant, from the standpoint of assimilation and integration, was the strength of cultural selection. So highly selective of "generational" classes was the incidence of segregation, or sitting-it-out in camp, and of outmigration, that these alternative resolutions of conflict may, without undue exaggeration, be called the Kibei way, the Issei way, and the Nisei way. Within each generational group, prewar residence, occupation, religion, and education, to a large extent, determined the course taken. Japanese Americans who had lived in the more tolerant Pacific Northwest were more frequently found in the salvage, those from more prejudiced California were disproportionately among the spoilage. Occupation, differentiating as it did the more isolated farming folk from those following urban pursuits where contact with the majority group was closer, stimulated salvage among the latter and retarded it among the former. Religion, too, differentiated cultural groups—the Japan-polarized Buddhists and Shintoists from the America-oriented who, like the white majority, either professed Christianity or accepted no formal religion. Segregation and sitting-it-out were the ways taken by the former; outmigration was the path of Christians and the a-religious. Finally, those who were most highly educated in American schools and colleges were—quite out of proportion to their numbers—the salvage.

III. 1950: A POSTSCRIPT

During 1945 and 1946, the evacuees began remigrating to the West Coast. The movement proceeded rapidly, and encompassed not only the bulk of the aging Issei and of the larger families, many of whose children had been born in camp, but also surprisingly large numbers of the Nisei who had left the camps and resettled in the Middle West and East, during the war years, and whom we have called "the salvage." By 1950, 80 per cent of the 141,000 persons of Japanese descent in the continental United States were living in the Western region, and 60 per cent of them were in California. The distribution of the demographic core of the salvage—persons who were 25–44 years of age in 1950 (survivors of the predominantly Nisei cohorts aged 15–34 in 1940)—followed the same pattern. Of the 46,000 persons in this age group, 35,000, or 76 per cent, were living in the Western region, and 27,000, or 59 per cent, were in California. However, approximately 7,500 (or 16 per cent of the total) had remained in or moved to the North Central region, most of them in the vicinity of Chicago; and 2,300 (or 5 per cent of the total) were living in or near New York City. The negligible remainder (less than 3 per cent of the total) was widely scattered throughout the southern states.

Within the severe limitations of 1950 census data on the Japanese minority, some light can be thrown on differences among these groups in respect to educational and occupational levels, and some questions can be raised regarding the selective aspects of their redistribution and their relative success in postwar adjustment.

The males of the core group, who returned or migrated to western cities, had approximately the same high level of education as the white residents (of the same age range) in the Los Angeles–San Francisco metropolitan areas, almost 30 per cent of both "racial" groups having entered or completed college; and among females of the same core group, the Japanese were only slightly disadvantaged compared with their white counterparts, the proportions being 18 and 24 per cent, respectively. Japanese who were, in 1950, residing in the North Central and eastern urban areas, however, had extraordinarily high educational levels, compared with whites in the metropolitan areas of Chicago and New

York. Among males, nearly half of the Japanese were college educated, compared to only about a quarter of the whites; and among females, too, the Japanese proportions were twice as high as were those for whites.

In Tables II and II–A, data for these several regional and racial groupings are presented for the core group aged 25–44 years, without further standardization for age. Those for the western grouping are roughly comparable with the data shown in Table I for California in the prewar period. Columns (1) and (2) in Table II, and the corresponding subtractions in Table II–A indicate the same general type and very much the same order of magnitude in the deviations of the nonagricultural occupational structure as before the war: deficiencies at the professional level; concentrations among unskilled laborers for males, and domestic servants for females; deficiencies among skilled laborers for males and in the clerical-sales category for females. The only noteworthy difference in prewar and postwar patterns is the disappearance, as of 1950, of the proprietor and clerical concentrations among males—which suggests, perhaps, the inability or unwillingness to re-establish ethnic enterprises.

The contrasts between distributions in the West, relative to distribution for whites, and those in the North Central and northeast are striking. In the North Central area, indeed, the distributions for both males and females are reasonably similar among Japanese and whites, with slight positive balances in the professions, slight negative balances in other white-collar occupations, and approximate equality at the levels of skilled and semiskilled labor. In the northeast, the high "indexes of dissimilarity" reflect concentration, especially for males, at the professional level, counterbalanced by deficiencies in almost all of the blue-collar occupations. From these distributions, alone, we may, therefore, draw the inference that those Japanese who returned to the West Coast had not improved their occupational status, to any marked extent, in the postwar period; that those who migrated to the Chicago area had found places for themselves in proportions roughly comparable to the white majority; and that those who were in the New York area contrasted as strongly with the whites as did the westerners but in

TABLE II. PERCENTAGE DISTRIBUTIONS BY OCCUPATION OF EMPLOYED LABOR FORCE 25–44 YEARS OF AGE, JAPANESE AND WHITES, BY SEX AND AREA OF RESIDENCE, 1950

Occupation	Japanese Western Urban (1)	Whites Los Angeles and San Francisco Metropolitan Area		Japanese North Central Urban (3)	Whites Chicago Metropolitan Area		Japanese Northeast Urban (5)	Whites New York and Northeastern New Jersey Metropolitan Area	
		(2)	Standardized to Education of Japanese (2a)		(4)	Standardized to Education of Japanese (4a)		(6)	Standardized to Education of Japanese (6a)
Males									
Professional	9.5	14.0	13.5	19.7	12.1	19.2	34.1	13.4	24.1
Proprietors, etc.	15.6	14.5	14.4	7.0	12.3	15.6	11.5	15.0	15.0
Clerical and sales	18.3	17.7	19.4	13.0	18.0	20.2	11.1	19.8	18.5
Craftsmen	11.0	24.5	21.9	25.5	24.5	19.1	14.4	19.6	17.4
Operatives	13.3	18.7	20.4	23.7	23.0	16.9	10.4	19.8	16.1
Service (except private household)	6.8	5.4	5.0	7.5	4.7	4.5	15.1	7.3	4.2
Private household workers	1.8	0.1	0.1	0.2	0.0	0.1	2.0	0.1	0.1
Laborers	23.7	5.1	5.3	3.4	5.4	4.4	1.4	5.0	4.6
Total	100.0	100.0	100.0	100.0	100.0	100.0	100.0	100.0	100.0
Females									
Professional	8.4	15.2	13.1	14.9	11.6	18.3	25.0	13.3	28.6
Proprietors, etc.	5.9	5.9	4.7	3.5	4.4	4.8	2.8	4.6	4.6
Clerical and sales	34.2	49.2	47.2	41.6	47.7	47.4	36.8	44.1	40.0
Craftsmen	0.9	1.7	1.7	2.3	2.5	1.6	0.4	2.1	1.4
Operatives	25.3	14.3	18.5	26.7	23.1	15.2	19.2	26.1	13.8
Service (except private household)	9.2	11.4	10.5	8.0	8.7	9.3	8.3	7.2	8.1
Private household workers	15.1	1.9	3.6	2.6	1.3	2.8	6.8	2.2	2.9
Laborers	1.0	0.4	0.7	0.4	0.7	0.6	0.7	0.4	0.6
Total	100.0	100.0	100.0	100.0	100.0	100.0	100.0	100.0	100.0

Source: Computed from data in U.S. Census of Population, 1950, as follows: Occupational and educational distributions of Japanese, aged 15–44, by sex and urban areas in Census regions, *Nonwhite Population by Race*, Table 11; occupational and educational distributions of whites, aged 15–44, by sex for standard metropolitan areas, *Characteristics of the Population*, State volumes, Tables 76 and 65.

Distributions of whites were standardized to the educational distribution of the Japanese by using percentage distributions of nonagricultural occupations by educational class, for ages 25–44, by sex for the total population in the North (North Central and Northeast) and West, derived from Special Census Report PE No. 5B on *Education*, Table 11.

TABLE II–A. DIFFERENCES BETWEEN PERCENTAGE DISTRIBUTIONS BY OCCU-
PATION OF EMPLOYED LABOR FORCE 25–44 YEARS OF AGE, JAPANESE AND
WHITES, BY SEX AND AREA OF RESIDENCE, 1950

(Numbers in column headings refer to Table II.)

Occupation	Western Urban, etc.		North Central Urban, etc.		Northeast Urban, etc.	
		Standardized for Education		Standardized for Education		Standardized for Education
	(1)–(2)	(1)–(2a)	(3)–(4)	(3)–(4a)	(5)–(6)	(5)–(6a)
Males						
Professional	− 4.5	− 4.0	+ 7.6	+ 0.5	+20.7	+10.0
Proprietors, etc.	+ 1.1	+ 1.2	− 5.3	− 8.6	− 3.5	− 3.5
Clerical and sales	+ 0.6	− 1.1	− 5.0	− 7.2	− 8.7	− 7.4
Craftsmen	−13.5	−10.9	+ 1.0	+ 6.4	− 5.2	− 3.0
Operatives	− 5.4	− 7.1	+ 0.7	+ 6.8	− 9.4	− 5.7
Service (except private household)	+ 1.4	+ 1.8	+ 2.8	+ 3.0	+ 7.8	+10.9
Private household workers	+ 1.7	+ 1.7	+ 0.2	+ 0.1	+ 1.9	+ 1.9
Laborers	+18.6	+18.4	− 2.0	− 1.0	− 3.6	− 3.2
Total	+23.4	+23.1	+12.3	+16.8	+30.4	+22.8
	−23.4	−23.1	−12.3	−16.8	−30.4	−22.8
Females						
Professional	− 6.8	− 4.7	+ 3.3	− 3.4	+11.7	− 3.6
Proprietors, etc.	0.0	+ 1.2	− 0.9	− 1.3	− 1.8	− 1.8
Clerical and sales	−15.0	−13.0	− 6.1	− 5.8	− 7.3	− 3.2
Craftsmen	− 0.8	− 0.8	− 0.2	+ 0.7	− 1.7	− 1.0
Operatives	+11.0	+ 6.8	+ 3.6	+11.5	− 6.9	+ 5.4
Service (except private household)	− 2.2	− 1.3	− 0.7	− 1.3	+ 1.1	+ 0.2
Private household workers	+13.2	+11.5	+ 1.3	− 0.2	+ 4.6	+ 3.9
Laborers	+ 0.6	+ 0.3	− 0.3	− 0.2	+ 0.3	+ 0.1
Total	+24.8	+19.8	+ 8.2	+12.2	+17.7	+ 9.6
	−24.8	−19.8	− 8.2	−12.2	−17.7	− 9.6

Source: Derived from Table II.

precisely the opposite direction, being notably concentrated at the
professional level.

If, now, we combine information about comparative educational
levels with that about comparative occupational levels, we can derive "population norms" to indicate the occupational distribution
that would be expected among the whites of this age group, if each
sex had the same educational level as that attained by the Japanese.
The proper comparison in Table II is, therefore, between columns
(1) and (2a) for the western region; between columns (3) and
(4a) for the North Central region; and between columns (5) and
(6a) for the northeastern region.

These comparisons are shown graphically in Figure 2. The corresponding subtractions in Table II–A indicate that standardization

for education had little effect on the discrepancies in the Western region, where the Japanese still had a markedly "unfavorable" distribution. In the North Central region, their professional density relative to the whites disappears for males and is reversed for females; and among males, there appears a greater concentration than expected among skilled and semiskilled laborers. In the northeast, too, the female disproportion in the professions disappears, but the achievement of males in attaining the levels for which their education had prepared them is still quite marked; and in neither the North Central nor the northeastern region is there any marked piling-up on the lowest rungs of the occupational ladder.

It would, of course, be rash to generalize these findings without analysis of the many facets of "minority status." By the single criterion of the occupational ladder, however, it seems evident that the highly educated Japanese Americans who remained outside the western area had moved, dramatically, out of minority occupational status; and that those who returned or migrated to the West were still in a markedly disadvantaged occupational position compared to the white majority.

The question as to why so many returned to the West is an unsolved puzzle. We suspect, however, that a number of noneconomic factors were involved in their decision. To most of the Issei and Nisei, as well as to many of the Kibei, California represented the homeland; the remainder of America was just as much a foreign country to them as Japan. And, once the movement had started, relatives and friends exerted a strong pull upon persons who had taken the lonely path of resettlement eastward during the war years.

Evidence of the strong positive selection in regard to education in outmigration from camps has been noted above, and is documented in much greater detail in *The Salvage*. This Postscript suggests that an even stronger selection may have operated to hold disproportionate numbers of the most highly educated resettlers in the cities of the Middle West and East. The persistence of a marked discrepancy between educational level and "expected" occupational structure in terms of this level in the West, contrasted with the favorable situation noted in the East, suggests a continued lag in the acceptance of the Japanese minority in the evacuation

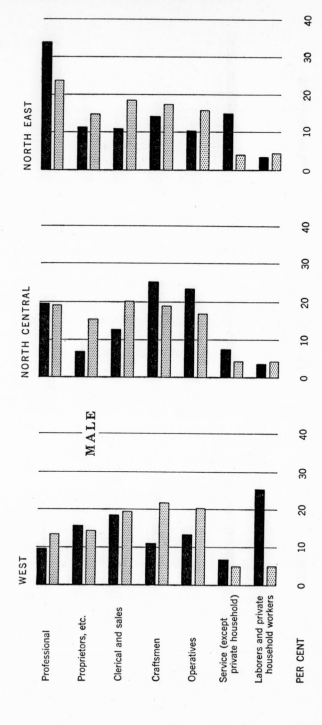

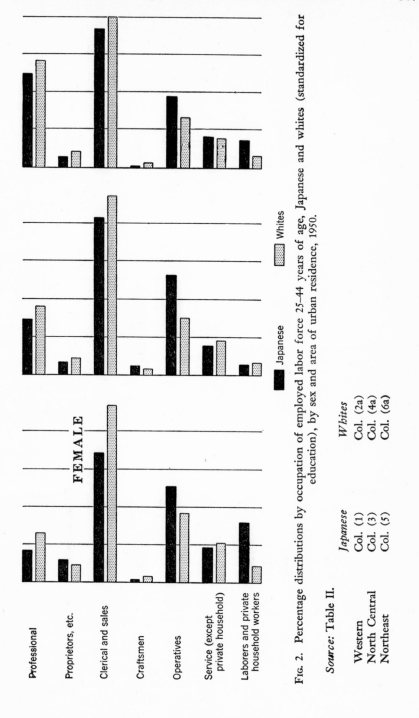

FEMALE

Professional

Proprietors, etc.

Clerical and sales

Craftsmen

Operatives

Service (except
private household)

Laborers and private
household workers

FIG. 2. Percentage distributions by occupation of employed labor force 25–44 years of age, Japanese and whites (standardized for education), by sex and area of urban residence, 1950.

Source: Table II.

	Japanese	Whites
Western	Col. (1)	Col. (2a)
North Central	Col. (3)	Col. (4a)
Northeast	Col. (5)	Col. (6a)

■ Japanese   ▦ Whites

area. In evaluating these interpretations, however, the comparative numbers involved should be held in mind, for they may well have been a factor of importance in the gain of status in the East and the failure to make similar gains in the West.

FOOTNOTES TO CHAPTER VI

1. Parts I and II of this chapter include some sections previously published by the writer in the *Proceedings of the American Philosophical Society*, Vol. 94 (1950), pp. 459–480, under the title "Some Social Aspects of Japanese-American Demography"; this article, in turn, was based on materials used in two volumes on the Japanese-American Evacuation and Resettlement issued by the University of California Press in 1946 (*The Spoilage*, by Dorothy Swaine Thomas and Richard S. Nishimoto), and in 1952 (*The Salvage*, by Dorothy Swaine Thomas, with the assistance of Charles Kikuchi and James Sakoda). The reader is referred to these publications for fuller documentation, for more detailed statistical analyses, and for more extensive bibliographical citations.

2. *Nisei* means, literally, "second generation," but the word is used to refer to American-born Japanese in general, including subsequent generations. In the California studies, we tried to preserve the distinction made by Japanese Americans by limiting use of the term to those of the American-born who were educated in American schools. *Kibei* (literally "returned to America") we similarly limit to those of the American-born who received some or all of their education in Japan.

3. E. K. Strong, Jr., R. Bell, *et al.*, *Vocational Aptitudes of Second-Generation Japanese in the United States*, especially pp. 81–113, 174–177, Stanford University Press, Stanford, Calif., 1933.

4. One in every two or three children born to Japanese immigrant parents was sent to Japan during the years between 1910 and 1930. Many of them remained in Japan; and the maximum density of Kibei among American-born evacuees as of 1942 was in the age range 25–29 years, where they represented 33 per cent.

5. As of 1942, the median age of Nisei was 17 years; of Kibei, 26 years; of Issei females, 47 years; and of Issei males, 55 years.

6. U.S. Army, Western Defense Command and Fourth Army, *Final Report: Japanese Evacuation from the West Coast, 1942*, pp. 33–38, 514, Washington, D.C., 1943.

7. *Ibid.*, p. 43.

8. Letter from M. S. Eisenhower to Budget Director Smith, May 11, 1942.

9. Opinion written by Judge William C. Mathes on August 27, 1948, in the U.S. District Court of Los Angeles; it was affirmed by Judge William Denman in the Court of Appeals.

10. In a document read to the evacuees in each camp by a member of the team conducting military registration in 1943.

CHAPTER VII

The Puerto Rican
in the United States

CLARENCE SENIOR

Puerto Rico became part of the United States in 1898, during the "manifest destiny" period of our economic and political expansion outside our continental area. It remained part of the "American Empire," without being consulted about it, until 1952. It became a Commonwealth and freely associated itself with the United States on July 25th of that year.[1] We are not now discussing the two and a quarter million people who live on the Caribbean island, which measures thirty-five miles wide and a hundred miles long. We are discussing those who have left that island to make their homes among us here.

The question "Why do they leave?" cannot be answered, however, without reference to the situation on the island as well as to the situation here.[2] The reasons are the same as those which impelled most of our forefathers, forty million strong, to come to our country: first, because they are needed, and, second, because they needed to come. They are needed in various parts of the United States in the same way that other internal migrants are needed, that is, because some parts of our economy are expanding more rapidly than others and thus need more workers. Students of labor economics in recent years have been stressing the great economic contribution made by the mobile section of our labor force. Such mobility helps tremendously in bringing about more uniform industrial development throughout the country.[3] Almost one in four of our citizens (23.5 per cent) now lives in other than his native state. Between April 1950 and April 1954 almost exactly sixteen million persons moved their homes across state boundaries;[4] 148,000 of them had been born in Puerto Rico, or a fraction of one per cent. Most of them came from other underdeveloped sections of the United States, primarily the South. They went where jobs were more readily available.

The only towns and cities which have not been experiencing an influx of migrants in recent years are the "ghost towns." An economy which is growing, or even one which is only replacing the workers who retire, die, shift to other occupations, or move from the city must always seek new persons for its "entry trades," at the bottom of the occupational ladder.[5]

The Puerto Rican migration from the island to the continent is economically oriented, just as was that of our forefathers and just as is the internal migration just mentioned. Data, available since 1908, show that the Puerto Rican migration has gone up as there was more of a demand for workers on the continent, has dropped when demand dropped, and has reversed its flow in the years of economic crisis.[6] The tightening of the job market which started in the fall of 1953 resulted in a drop of 68.8 per cent from 1953 to 1954 in the Puerto Rican migration, for example. The net migration for the past ten years has been 403,869, or an average of 40,387 per year. The yearly net flow from 1945 to 1954 was as follows.

1945	13,573	1950	34,703
1946	39,911	1951	52,900
1947	24,551	1952	59,103
1948	38,775	1953	69,124
1949	25,698	1954	21,531

The need for workers in the continental United States is what students of migration call the "pull." The situation in Puerto Rico is known as the "push." The first is pretty obvious and has always been the major factor in either internal migration or international emigration. The second may lead to some misunderstanding. Therefore, we need a cursory glance at the Puerto Rican economy.

"Operation Bootstrap"

The Puerto Rican economy has, in the recent past, become one of the most-studied and most-commented-upon in modern history. "Operation Bootstrap" has excited the interest and admiration of the underdeveloped two thirds of the world to such an extent that the government of the Commonwealth created a Technical Assistance Office to cope with the stream of visitors flocking to the island from all parts of the globe to see for themselves what is being done to speed up the process of economic and social reconstruction. The Foreign Operations Administration recently signed a contract with the Commonwealth to use Puerto Rico as a worldwide demonstration center in the techniques of developing underdeveloped areas.

Many of the advances made in recent years can be expressed exactly, in statistical form. Expectancy of life, for example, has been pushed up from 46 years at birth in 1940 to 62 years in 1955. If no other data were available on the rapid rise in levels of living, this comparison alone would suffice to prove what dramatic gains have been achieved. There are many other data, however.

A rise in life expectancy is, of course, only another way of expressing a reduction in the death rate. The death rate itself has been cut down from 18.4 per 1000 in 1940 to 7.7 in 1954, a rate which is lower than that for the continental United States, partly because of the much higher proportion of the Puerto Rican population in the younger ages.

The very difference in the age structure proves to be one of Puerto Rico's major handicaps. A population in which death rates are dropping rapidly but birth rates continue high is inevitably overburdened by the support of these who are not "earning their keep." They must be supported by the economy to which they, as yet, contribute nothing. A major item in the cost of such support is the educational system. Puerto Rico must support about twice as great a proportion of its population under age sixteen as does the mainland.

Education is a vital factor not only in economic, political, and cultural development, but also makes a major contribution toward securing an application of intelligence to the control of births as well as deaths. Generally, the Puerto Rican mother with no schooling averages six children; one with a grade school education, or better, averages 3.[7] The biggest single obstacle to family planning anywhere in the world is still ignorance of the existence of any alternative to continuous childbearing, except abortion. There are now one hundred and sixty infant and maternal welfare clinics in Puerto Rico at which advice on family planning is available. The birth rate is beginning to drop, even though much more slowly than the death rate.[8] The decrease in the death rate from 1940 to 1954 was 58.2 per cent; but the fall in the birth rate was only 11.1 per cent. The result is a rate of natural increase of 2.7 per cent per year, which is almost triple the rate of natural increase between 1900 and 1904, 1 per cent.[9] This rate means somewhat over 60,000 persons a year are added to a population which already has reached a density of 650 per square mile, compared with the density of the continental United States of 50 per square mile.

Such density forces the Puerto Rican economy to support relatively thirteen times the number of people per square mile supported by our enormously richer mainland economy. It is as though the state of New Jersey (with approximately the same population density) were to try to support its people by farming alone instead of by agriculture, industry, commerce, and services.

The per capita income of the Puerto Rican people has been pushed up from $122 per year in 1940 to $432 in 1954. This puts Puerto Rico ahead of all the Latin American republics but three: Argentina, Uruguay, and Venezuela. Even so, this is only about one fifth that of the continental United States and one half that of its poorest state, Mississippi.

Unemployment has been reduced by one third in the past dozen years and underemployment even more drastically. The government's industrialization program has brought 342 new industrial plants to the island and has increased measureably the number of workers in secondary and service jobs. Unemployment remains a threat to the whole economy, however, with 72,000 out of work in 1954 in a labor force of 631,000. This represents 11.4 per cent of the labor force, or about three times the proportion out of work on the mainland in the same year.

Those who are employed are significantly better off than they have ever been previously. [The past decade has seen incomes rise at a rate varying from 19 per cent in transportation and public utilities to 326 per cent in construction.] Puerto Rico is now, per capita, one of the best offshore customers of the mainland United States; in 1953 it purchased about $500,000,000 of goods, or an average of $1,369,000 every day in the year. Included in this is about half of the food consumed on the island, in spite of intensive efforts to diversify and modernize agriculture.[10]

All of this adds up to an economy full of vitality, to a culture which, after four-and-a-half centuries of colonialism, has worked out new solutions for old problems. It is proud to live in fraternal association with the United States; the people overwhelmingly have indicated time and again how deeply they value their common citizenship with us.

That there is an important change in the quality of life on the island seems to this observer to be indicated, among other things, by the drop of almost half in the suicide rate in the past decade: from 20.6 per 1000 in 1943 to 11.2 in 1953. The homicide rate has dropped even more dramatically: from 16.4 to 6.7. These data certainly do not indicate that Puerto Rico is "hopeless and helpless," which is part of the stereotype about the island in the minds of so many continental Americans.

WHY DO PUERTO RICANS MIGRATE?

Why then, if conditions are improving so well, do Puerto Ricans leave their island and come to the continental United States? Ambition and hope, added to differential job opportunities, make up the three major ingredients in voluntary migration. The process of economic development (which always includes education as a *sine qua non*) raises hopes in the hearts of the more ambitious. They are the ones who are attracted by the greater opportunities in areas in which there is *more rapid* economic expansion. An indication of how this works is given by a comparison of the skilled, semiskilled and unskilled members in the labor force of Puerto Rico and of the migration. Skilled workers make up only five per cent of the labor force in Puerto Rico, but eighteen per cent of the migrant labor force, a difference of more than three times. The semiskilled account for twenty per cent of the Puerto Rican labor force but more than twice that in the migrant labor force. The unskilled make up half of the Puerto Rican labor force, but only twenty-one per cent of the labor force among the migrants. Many other examples could be given of the selective process in the migration. Overwhelmingly (in eighty-five per cent of the cases) the migrants in the labor force had quit jobs on the island to make the trip; only fifteen per cent had been unemployed at the time they left Puerto Rico. In other words, the migrants do not come in search of jobs as such, but of *better* jobs.[11]

Thus we find that the Puerto Rican migrants come for the same reasons most of our ancestors came. The resemblance does not stop here. The Puerto Rican, in spite of his American citizenship, is a "stranger in a strange land." English is a foreign tongue to about half of the migrants. Many customs are different, and his attitudes often diverge widely from the norms of the host society. The parallels between the experience of our ancestors, as set forth so brilliantly in Oscar Handlin's Pulitzer Prize-winning book, *The Uprooted*,[12] are many and close. Obviously, I am speaking of the lives of the "hewers of wood and drawers of water" and not of such Puerto Ricans as José Ferrer and Juano Hernandez in the movies and on the stage; or Jesus Maria Sanromá, the soloist for the Boston Symphony Orchestra at one end of the scale, or Noro Morales, the composer and orchestra leader on the other; or the brilliant lawyer Felipe N. Torres, member of our state assembly from the Bronx; or Rubén Gómez in baseball, or many others who have earned enviable reputations in business or the professions.

One of the dangers of talking about "the Puerto Rican," "the Negro," etc., is that it helps the unthinking person judge the whole group on the basis of a few experiences with individual members of the group. Quite often I am told that "so-and-so doesn't look like a Puerto Rican." We know from anthropological studies that only eleven per cent of the Swedes "look like Swedes." I have heard tourists in Italy remark that they had traveled down the northern two thirds of the Italian peninsula before they found people who "looked like Italians." Generalizing from insufficient data is one of the oldest of logical fallacies.

Culture Conflict

This does not mean that we must agree with the French cynic that "all generalizations are false, including this one." Puerto Ricans, like most other ethnic groups, differ from one another according to the class from which they come, their age, sex, education, the locality on the island where they were born and raised, their skin color, their previous experience, and many other factors. However, there are certain situations which arise more often than others, and there are areas of misunderstanding which are relatively common. Most of them involve what sociologists call "culture conflict." Essentially, this revolves around the idea that what is required in a particular situation is obvious to persons brought up in one culture but may be looked upon as irrelevant, silly, or harmful by persons from another culture. The very word "outlandish," used by many persons to describe actions which are beyond the pale of understanding, has its origin in those things done by foreigners ("outlanders").

For example, in Puerto Rico when relatives meet they are expected to embrace. This is a gesture required by the culture of most Puerto Ricans. Those reflexes often survive in spite of a change in the circumstances which gave rise to them. A well-dressed, upper middle class Puerto Rican woman checking into an expensive hotel in New York City last year did not hesitate to throw her arms around the bell captain in the lobby when she recognized him as a first cousin. The bell captain was discharged for "being familiar with a woman guest." Similar instances of misunderstanding arising out of automatic reactions could be multiplied by the thousands. The major fields in which they are most likely to be found may be indicated in a series of contrasts between the culture of the Puerto Rican before he leaves the island and that of the area into which he moves. Individual Puerto Ricans may react in several different ways to the adjustment process which is required, but it is still a strain on most of them.

SMALL TOWN VS. METROPOLITAN PATTERNS

The average migrant to New York and other urban areas comes from Puerto Rican cities, but these still are small towns compared with the great cities of the continental United States.

New York City life, particularly, is a peak of urbanism. Social contacts are transitory and impersonal. Community control has given way to impersonal, institutionalized controls. The individual is anonymous to most of his fellow-beings. Time is measured by the second-hand of the watch. Sanitation is a highly organized machinery involving thousands of persons and costing thousands of dollars an hour. The small shop in the old home town becomes in the new city a plant with thousands of workers. The short bus ride turns into a subway juggernaut packed with human beings, to each of whom life seems to depend on forcing himself into a particular car.

The population density of 660 per square mile in Puerto Rico is great in the setting of its economy. But the migrant is still utterly unprepared for the 85,905 persons per square mile on the island of Manhattan.

While discrimination exists in Puerto Rico, it is limited largely to the inherited attitudes of upper-class Spaniards. Puerto Ricans seldom judge a person's ability by the color of his skin. But when they move to New York, from an environment in which Spaniards and Negroes have lived together for several hundred years without serious race conflict, they suddenly discover an atmosphere charged with the feeling that a white skin means innate superiority.

Thus they learn the meaning of a color line, by which people are classified as Negro or as white. If a Puerto Rican has too dark a skin, too kinky hair, or broad features, he is almost sure to be typed and discriminated against in exactly the same way as an American Negro. His whole security as a person may suddenly be threatened. Fear of prejudice and exclusion may influence him to retain his own language and customs in order to differentiate himself. At the same time, he may try to remain inside the boundaries of a Puerto Rican neighborhood in order to escape discriminatory racial patterns. But thereby he is also prevented from learning the ways of the more widespread and older populations of the city. A still more insidious and dangerous symptom of his fear may be complete rejection of the American Negro, with its inevitable corollaries of hostility and bitterness.

STATUS VS. COMPETITION

Caste and class lines must also be considered. The Puerto Rican is born into a status from which he seldom changes. Spanish ancestry or American money are the two chief determinants of upper-class status, although strata lines are being increasingly crossed with the spread of free education and other democratic practices.

In New York, as well as in the rest of Western industrial civilization, competition for status is acute. Although the Puerto Rican enters the competitive market at the bottom, he, too, is expected to "work his way to the top." Thereby, he may suffer the same neurotic damage that commonly afflicts other members of our acquisitive society. As Dr. Karen Horney points out:

> From its economic center competition radiates into all other activities and permeates love, social relations and play. Therefore, competition is a problem for everyone in our culture, and it is not at all surprising to find it an unfailing center of neurotic conflicts.

The Puerto Rican migrant suffers even more than mainland citizens, however. In addition to the disabilities already mentioned, his own cultural background is far less acquisitive and competitive than the strange new one he has just entered. It stresses more the enjoyment of life through poetry, music, dancing, and the esthetic generally, rather than through the accumulation of money.

CONTROL VS. FREEDOM

The extent of personal freedom is another contrast. In Puerto Rico, the conflict between the older patriarchal pattern of the Spanish family and the emerging democratic pattern of participation by wife and children in family decisions and actions may be a serious one. Nevertheless, the right of woman to work and "have her say" about family matters and the right of children neither to be ruled with an iron hand nor smothered by over-affection are slowly gaining acceptance in Puerto Rico.

In coming to New York, the Puerto Rican housewife discovers a still greater freedom—sometimes not without disrupting effects. While only a fourth of the women in Puerto Rico are gainfully employed, Manhattan presents the sharp contrast of about half the women working. The average husband, whether grudgingly or not, accepts the reality that he will be better off when his wife is able to make money. In many instances, however, the family pattern is thereby upset. Children receive less attention from the mother—sometimes much too little, with all the negative consequences of maladjustment, insecurity, delinquency. The woman realizes that she is no longer so dependent. She can threaten to leave her husband, if he becomes despotic, and count on relatively greater future security than if she were in Puerto Rico.

The new environment is especially puzzling and frustrating to the adolescent. If he belongs to a closely united and strongly governed family, he is allowed only limited freedom by his parents. Both boys and girls thus quickly sense the differences between their own family traditions and those of many of their associates in neighborhood groups, high schools, or churches. Depending, again, on the total family situation and how the environment affects it, the Puerto Rican adolescent is confronted with a range of bewildering possibilities, so that it is impossible to know how he will react—whether by passive obedience, frustration, or outright rebellion.

Family ties create still another problem. Puerto Ricans feel unusually responsible for their relatives and often take them all into their own home, regardless of the facilities available. This loyalty is so strong, indeed, that it frequently leads to misunderstanding in other groups where such familiar solidarity is no longer the rule. For example, labor union officials have told me about girls who turn their working cards over to their sisters when they themselves are ill so that their sisters may earn a day's wages in that way. Hospital administrators tell me that members of families are so concerned with the health of one particular member that often the entire family shows up in the hospital waiting room when only one member has an appointment for a medical examination.

Naturally, the personnel of large institutions such as hospitals and labor unions find it irritating and even frustrating when their clients act in such an "outlandish" manner. It is natural also that the Puerto Ricans involved may not know "what all the shouting is about" when their actions give rise to unfamiliar and sometimes hostile reactions.

LANGUAGE

Adjustment, it should be understood, must always be a two-way process. There must be communication between the older resident and the newcomer. Millions of our forefathers had the same trouble as does the Puerto Rican who doesn't speak English. "But why doesn't the Puerto Rican speak English?" The answer is far from simple. First, it should be noted that the role of English in the Puerto Rican schools has often caused bitter controversy between Washington and San Juan. English was the official teaching language over half the time from 1898 to 1949 in spite of the fact that Spanish is the language of the people. It is easy to imagine what chaos existed in the school system, for instance, when thousands of teachers, imported from the continental United States, tried to teach students whom they could not understand and who could not understand them. The results of that policy, in the words of the present Commissioner of Education, were

> the obvious ones of lack of progress in both English and the subject taught; a tendency to memorize by rote without understanding; discouragement with the whole learning process; and a prejudice against English as the cause of the whole trouble.

The colonial aspect of language and the resentment which the policy created cannot be ignored, particularly in the case of adults who may have some emotional trouble in the learning of English. Fortunately, the removal of all but traces of colonialism in the relationship between Washington and the Puerto Ricans is contributing greatly to helping speed up the process of learning English on the island. A great step ahead was made on January 2, 1949, at the inauguration of the first governor ever to be elected by the Puerto Rican people themselves. His first official act was the appointment of the first Puerto Rican Commissioner of Education ever to control the educational system of the island, either under Spain or under the United States. In turn, the new Commissioner's first official act was to announce that, although Spanish was to be the medium of instruction, the teaching of English would be intensified. The action met with widespread popular support and has removed one of the psychological blocks against the English language.

There is an additional factor on the island itself which must now be taken into account, since the psychological blocks have largely been removed. It was noted above that Puerto Rico spends a large share of its income on education; actually it is four times what we spend in the continental United States, proportionately. It must be added that, in spite of this, the school system still needs three thousand additional classrooms in order to put all children of school age in school. While the schools are now teaching English more widely and more effectively than they ever did before, the children of Puerto Ricans moving to the continent may still have had inadequate general schooling.

One additional factor must be considered to round out our treatment of the language problem. In a study made by Columbia University it was found that there was high correlation between a dark complexion and continued use of Spanish. Puerto Ricans who face prejudice and discrimination may use their native language as a shield to protect themselves against the treatment we accord the American Negro.

Our Metropolitan Problems

Those Puerto Ricans who move to large urban areas land in the midst of a complex of problems which now concern civic-minded persons in every metropolitan area. Our large cities have been "decaying at the center" for many years. The central city of every metropolitan area is either declining in population or its population growth is exceedingly slow in comparison with that of suburban areas. This is an accompaniment of the increased social mobility of the last few years, and it interlocks with the geographical mobility which has brought various new ethnic groups to metropolitan areas. The Puerto Rican, like other recent working-class arrivals, has nowhere to go except into what are sometimes euphemistically called "deteriorated neighborhoods." That this is a great disadvantage for him and his family is obvious. His family becomes one with the six million American families now living in the slums of our big cities. He may become the victim of a handful of speculators such as those who in Brooklyn, for example, have been reaping profits of at least $500,000 a year by purchasing run-down properties at about assessed valuations and reselling them at two or three times the purchase price under installment contracts involving in some cases as many as three or four mortgages. Purchasers, according to one New York City investigation, have been advised to occupy small parts of the premises and let the remaining space at weekly rentals to individuals or families as "roomers," thereby obtaining total monthly incomes far greater than could be obtained by renting apartments on a monthly basis.[13]

These matters are well known to most sophisticated persons in the big cities through public investigations; they are well known through bitter experience to the recent arrivals in the big cities.

What is even more bitter, sometimes, is that the conditions of which the newcomer is a victim are laid at his door. The process of the "emptying out of the central city" into the suburbs has been taking place for years irrespective of the ethnic groups involved. The natural history of urban neighborhoods shows a continuous decline which begins to speed up fifty or seventy-five years after most of the houses were built. The decline usually is so gradual and the replacement of older populations by newer populations so unspectacular that older residents often are unaware of the process. However, when members of minority groups which in one way or another are more highly "visible" than the rest of the population move into a neighborhood, the newcomer becomes a symbol of the decline of the neighborhood and therefore is blamed for the decline.[14]

A look at the situation in public housing developments in New York City will throw some light on the Puerto Ricans as "good housekeepers." The secretary of the New York City Housing Authority told the Welfare Council of New York in 1953 that, in the estimate of the managers of New York City Housing Authority projects, "the housekeeping habits of Puerto Ricans are above average." The rent payment record was the same as that of other groups. The Puerto Rican children "treat property better than those of most other ethnic groups." The same thing is reported from all over the United States about most other minority groups in the stream of internal migration. Decent housing and neighborhood cooperation can usually be counted upon to speed up the adjustment process tremendously.

DIFFERENCES TODAY

Parallels between the Puerto Rican migration and the immigration of the past have been stressed up to this point. There are differences which should be mentioned. One of the most important is the fact that it has now been three decades since there was any sizeable immigration to the United States. In that thirty years, many of the settlement houses and group work agencies which specialized in helping speed up the process of adjustment of newcomers to the community, and of the community to the newcomer, have gone out of existence or their personnel has changed to such an extent that they were no longer in a position to help the non-English-speaking stranger. The older citizen and the established institutions are quite often puzzled and frustrated by the discrepancies between the legal status of Puerto Ricans as citizens of the United States, proud enough of their heritage to leave an inordinately large number of dead volunteers on the battlefields of Korea, and their speaking a strange language and carrying with them a strange culture. Many persons usually not given to displays of xenophobia seem to be aroused by this anomaly.

There are two differences on the credit side of the ledger. First, the work of the social scientists has given men and women of good will perspective, insight, and techniques which were denied the personnel of community institutions in helping the adjustment process in the days of great waves of immigration. It is encouraging to note that the constantly refined tools of social research are, on the whole, proving what the great spirits of Jane Addams, Lillian Wald, Paul U. Kellogg, Mary Simkovitch, Jacob Riis, and others knew from their experience and their deep understanding of the wellsprings of human behavior. They worked out the goal which has only recently been labeled "cultural democracy" and which I believe is one of the most magnificent concepts to be formulated in the history of the human race.[15]

Second, his government is helping the Puerto Rican help himself when he comes to the continental United States. The Commonwealth government neither encourages nor, usually, discourages migration. It does undertake an orientation program at home. Part of this orientation may consist in warning the Puerto Rican that jobs are scarce on the continent, which is exactly what it did in the fall of 1953 when the "rolling adjustment" began. Orientation at home takes place via radio, pamphlets, films, the school system, newspaper releases, interviews, speeches, and in the eight local offices of the Puerto Rico Employment Service. Special stress is always placed upon the desirability of knowing a modicum of English.

A "Migration Division" is maintained in the states, with offices in New York City and in the Middle West and a national staff which operates outside those areas. It operated in one hundred and fifteen communities last year, which gives some idea of the dispersion of the Puerto Ricans. It works closely on both farm and industrial programs with the United States Employment Service and with affiliated state agencies. It thus has weekly and monthly reports of job opportunities available throughout the United States and the help of local employment service offices in working out arrangements with employers and community agencies. The Migration Division helps employers in such matters as the preparation of plant-in-training manuals, safety manuals and posters, and in clearing up misunderstandings which may develop in the early days of the employment of Puerto Ricans. In addition to its employment service, it maintains a staff of social workers, educational consultants, and community organization specialists so that both the Puerto Rican and the communities into which he moves are aided. The work of the Migration Division in helping the Puerto Ricans help themselves has been aided considerably in recent years by the success of various aspects of "Operation Bootstrap," but particularly that of the Community Education Division of the Puerto Rican Department of Education. Its films, pamphlets, leaflets, and scientific studies all concentrate on the idea of cooperation for the common good. They are constantly used in Puerto Rican communities on the continent, with increasing success.

SIGNIFICANCE OF THE PUERTO RICANS

I have been discussing what is, in either absolute or relative terms, a small group. The 2,250,000 people of Puerto Rico are but a tiny fraction of the 2,500,000,000 people in the world, or even of the 164,000,000 people who are citizens of the United States. Puerto Ricans living on the continent, first and second generation, do not exceed 750,000. Professor Collier pointed out in his discussion of the American Indians that even the comparatively small group of 400,000 native Americans has a great significance to us and to our times. The same is true of the Puerto Ricans.

First, we badly need a bridge of understanding between us and the 170,000,000 persons living in the Latin American republics. Puerto Rico, having had an opportunity to choose the best of the Spanish culture and the best of our culture, is in a position to help us develop that bridge.

We also need bridges of understanding between us and the millions of people in the world who live in "underdeveloped" or in colonial areas of the world. Puerto Rico has been helping tremendously as a laboratory for technical assistance and, as many speakers at the United Nations remarked, Puerto Rico in working out its commonwealth status may well serve as a guiding light for many other colonies torn between the Scylla of continued colonial dependence and the Charybdis of an independence which would wreck their economies.

The Puerto Rican who comes to live among us is not only serving as a significant addition to the labor force on the farms and railroads and in the factories; he is also giving us an opportunity to begin equipping ourselves and our children successfully to play the role which our economic development has thrust upon us. Most educated people pay verbal tribute to the "one world" concept, but the important National Planning Association a few years ago stated that the United States is "a giant in world power and an infant in world perspective." [16] The presence of this new group of strangers among us gives us an opportunity to start, in our own backyard, putting our "one world" ideals into practical operation.

FOOTNOTES TO CHAPTER VII

1. See Luis Muñoz Marín, "Development Through Democracy," and other articles in the political development section of *The Annals of the American Academy of Political and Social Science*, V. 285, Jan. 1953; and "Puerto Rico and the United States, Their Future Together," *Foreign Affairs*, July 1954, pp. 541–551.

2. See Earl Parker Hanson, *Transformation: the Story of Modern Puerto Rico*, Simon & Schuster, New York, 1955.

3. E. Wight Bakke *et al.*, *Labor Mobility and Economic Opportunity*, John Wiley & Sons, New York, 1954.

4. "Current Population Reports," Series P-20, no. 57, Apr. 1955, Bureau of the Census, Washington, D.C.

5. A. J. Jaffe, "Puerto Rican Population of New York City," pp. 3–29, Bureau of Applied Social Research, Columbia University, New York, 1954.

6. Harvey Perloff, *Puerto Rico's Economic Future*, ch. 13, University of Chicago Press, Chicago, 1950.

7. Lydia J. Roberts and Rosa L. Stefani, *Patterns of Living in Puerto Rican Families*, pp. 26–27, Rio Piedras, University of Puerto Rico, 1949; Paul K. Hatt, *Backgrounds of Human Fertility in Puerto Rico*, 512 pp., Princeton University Press, Princeton, 1952.

8. J. Mayone Stycos and Reuben Hill, "The Prospects of Birth Control in Puerto Rico," *The Annals of the American Academy of Political and Social Science*, V. 285, Jan. 1953, pp. 137–144.

9. Recent data from "Facts and Figures," Migration Division, Puerto Rico Department of Labor, New York, 1955 (mimeographed).

10. Nathan Koenig, *A Comprehensive Agricultural Program for Puerto Rico*, pp. 299, Washington, D.C., 1953.

11. C. Wright Mills, Clarence Senior, and Rose Goldsen, 288 pp., *The Puerto Rican Journey*, Harper and Brothers, New York, 1950; Clarence Senior, "Migration and Economic Development," *Journal of Educational Sociology*, Dec. 1954, pp. 151–156.

12. 310 pp., Little, Brown & Co., Boston, 1952.

13. New York *Times*, October 26, 1953, and November 21, 1953; "Report of Mayor's Committee on Housing," City Hall, New York, 1955 (mimeographed); Charles F. Palmer, *Adventures of a Slum Fighter*, 272 pp., Tupper and Love, Atlanta, 1955.

14. Charles Abrams, "The New 'Gresham's Law of Neighborhoods'—Fact or Fiction," *The Appraisal Journal*, V. xix, July 1951, pp. 324–337.

15. See various contributions in *One America*, 764 pp., ed. by Francis J. Brown and Joseph S. Roucek, Prentice-Hall, New York, 1952.

16. *America's New Opportunities in World Trade*, p. 73, National Planning Association, Washington, 1944.

CHAPTER VIII

Understanding
Minority Groups

JOSEPH B. GITTLER

In this Institute, we have been confronted by one of the most pressing social problems of modern times, a problem which in essence deals with the organization of society both in this country and around the world. As we study our own nation and other nations as well, we find this problem of minority-majority group relations emerging in one form or another. It may wear many masks, but underneath it has the same features.

This has been brought home to us most forcibly by the previous essays. As each writer dealt with some facet of this subject, it became clear, I believe, that we have not adjusted our social behavior to our social needs. One of the crucial questions of contemporary life is: "How can men live together peacably, productively, and harmoniously in the kind of society we have inherited today?" Because we have given little heed to this question we found, throughout this series of papers, evidences of discrimination of many kinds—prejudice against and intolerance of people simply because they belong to groups other than our own.

126

We have surveyed certain ethnic groups, certain religious groups, certain color groups, and we noted that whatever group we studied, there tended to be a barrier of some kind between the particular group and other groups. Sometimes this barrier was thinly veiled; in other instances the barrier was deep and high. The barrier, however, was always the result of the attitudes and actions of others toward these groups. In all these instances of difference there were concomitant factors of prejudice and discrimination.

It is these concepts of prejudice and discrimination that furnish us with the clue to the concept of minority groups. Here I should like to digress for a few moments and clarify our definition of minority groups and the way we have used the concept. It is important to remember that when we seek knowledge about a phenomenon, that phenomenon can be known only through an assumed frame of reference. We cannot know everything about anything; we can only know about something from a particular frame of reference. Thus a minority group means one thing from a statistical and numerical standpoint; it may mean quite another from a social-interhuman frame of reference. From an intergroup, interhuman frame of reference numbers are not necessarily significant in determining minority group status. (It may affect the status but does not determine it.)

Let me illustrate. There are counties in the South where Negroes substantially outnumber the whites. In South Africa, the whites are relatively few in number as compared with those of other races. In many colonial outposts, a handful of whites dominated millions of non-whites. Yet we often refer to these relationships as majority-minority group problems. Obviously we are indicating a pattern of relationship in the distribution of prestige, power, and privilege, rather than a numerical relationship.

Accordingly, we look upon a minority group as a social collectivity of persons who,

> because of their physical or cultural characteristics, are singled out from the others in the society in which they live for differential and unequal treatment, and who regard themselves as objects of collective discrimination. The existence of a minority in a society implies the existence of a corresponding dominant group with higher social status and greater privileges. Minority status carries with it the exclusion from full participation in the life of the society.[1]

If we keep this concept of a minority group in mind, I believe we can more readily understand that the problems surrounding group relations do not consist of the *actual differences between groups*, but rather in the way we *react to these differences*. If the reaction is one of prejudice and discrimination and leads to the social subordination of any groups, these groups are said to have minority status.

There are many definitions of prejudice. Prejudice will be used here as meaning the emotional and rigid tendency to prejudge and misjudge human groups in a hostile fashion. Prejudice as an attitude should be distinguished from discrimination as overt action. Prejudice may not translate itself into action against members of a minority group. There may be many situations where such prejudices find little opportunity for expression, or where the social climate prohibits the open expression of hostility. Thus prejudice must not be equated with discrimination.

Nevertheless, they are closely related. There are situations where we find attitudes of prejudice but no discrimination; conversely, we see forms of discrimination without prejudice. In general, we find both mutually strengthening each other.

In intergroup relations the dominant group usually tends to have certain prevailing biases or prejudices toward the given minority. There always seems to be a strong in-group sense of superiority, and along with this feeling an implicit attitude that the dominant group has an inherent right to certain privileges, advantages, and opportunities. With these attitudes, we also find a sense that the minority group is alien and strange and offers a threat to the majority group in certain areas. All of these attitudes are self-explanatory and need little analysis here. Each of us examining his own attitudes will probably find some elements of these feelings. Further, if we listen carefully to discussions on desegregation in schools or in housing, for example, we will find many of the arguments falling into each of these categories.

These feelings are the basic material of prejudicial attitudes. If these feelings of hostility give rise to open acts of "againstness," taking various forms, we have prejudice aligning itself with discrimination—i.e., "the deliberate holding down of the minority group." [2]

It should be understood that in the context of this analysis we do not use the word "discrimination" as it is popularly used. When we use the term discrimination in intergroup relations, we are not referring to the ability to recognize distinctions and express individual tastes and preferences. Discrimination in intergroup relations denotes dominant group opposition to members of minority groups. The opposition usually takes the form of disallowing the same or equivalent opportunities afforded to members of dominant groups.

It should not be construed that we fail to recognize the importance to individuals and to groups of their own value systems and ideologies. Men live by their convictions, but there is overwhelming evidence that most forms of discrimination are not based on valid and rational objection to a minority group's values or ideologies, but on prejudice and bias. Numerous studies have indicated that many of those who are most violently prejudiced toward given minority groups either know little about the groups, or what they think they know tends to be highly inaccurate. It is feasible for men of good will to hold honest differences of opinion, conviction, and faith. In a nation nurtured by the Bill of Rights, the Constitution, and the recognition of the inherent dignity and worth of the individual, it seems unnecessary and a violation of our basic code to have such honest differences find expression in hatred, violence, discrimination, and patent injustice.

Each of the previous writers described for us the experiences of prejudices and discrimination suffered by a particular minority group and how the group responded to these forces. Most of these groups have had a long history involving prejudice and discrimination. Each generation of the minority group tended to inherit a sharp awareness of this history from the previous generation. This awareness, heightened by personal experience, frequently has had a tremendous impact on the personality development of individuals within the minority group.

We have learned much from the work of scholars like William James, John Dewey, Jean Piaget, Charles Horton Cooley, George Herbert Mead, and a host of others, about the ways in which a child forms basic attitudes toward himself, toward the values of his own group, and those of the larger society. These facets of his personality develop from his contact with others, from the ways they define his roles, and from the manner in which he is encouraged to see himself—all, of course, conditioned by his inherited tendencies and previous experiences. In Cooley's phrase, we have a "looking-glass self" made up of others' reactions to us, our interpretation of those reactions, and the response to the interpretation. George Herbert Mead has said we know ourselves only "by taking the role of the other"—by reacting to ourselves as we imagine others react to us. In time we learn to take the role of the "generalized other"—the norms of society and the groups to which we belong. We come to see ourselves in the light of these norms or standards.

Such a process is significantly different for the members of a minority group than for the members of a dominant group. In American society, a high proportion of non-Caucasian children come to see themselves as somehow different from white children —unable to do certain things, to go to certain places, frequently rebuffed by words and gestures. From childhood to death, many minority group members are likely to experience a long series of events ranging from exclusion from play groups and cliques to violence and the threat of violence. These are far less likely to be experienced by the average member of the dominant group.

Not all of these experiences are necessarily "bad" or unfortunate. A minority group member's difficulties may lead to achievement, to a kind of "challenge-response" situation, to use Arnold Toynbee's phrase. Some of the notable contributions of minority group members to art, to religion, to science may have been achieved *because of their difficulties*, not simply in spite of them. The artistry of a Marian Anderson, the insight of a Richard Wright, the wisdom of an Albert Einstein, can perhaps partially be explained in this way. Deprivation can lead to understanding; suffering can produce great personal warmth and sympathy for others. Such results, however, do not appear to be the most common. The great weight of prejudice and discrimination frequently twists and distorts the development of personality in the minority group member. Often his experience leads him into conflict situations which put him at odds with himself and with his world.

Lillian Smith reports her conversation with the young secretary to the President of a Negro college in the South:

She was a lovely thing to look at, quiet, poised, and I found her face more interesting than the buildings and spacious gardens. We walked near the entrance that led to the street and stood, watching a street-car pass by toward the "white" section of town. And then we turned back toward the library. I said, "It is beautiful in here, peaceful, quiet. I find it hard to remember the world out there that I will go back to tomorrow." She did not answer for a moment, then she said softly, "I wish I never had to go out there, even to shop. I would like never to go. In here, one forgets; you can believe you are a real person. You go out there and they tear it off you, your belief in yourself as something good, they tear it off in five minutes. It doesn't take much, a word you hear a man say, a glance, someone draws aside, that is all; a clerk in a store asks you your first name as if she cannot otherwise sell you a pair of shoes. Little things. . . . And suddenly you are untouchable. In here . . . sometimes for a month, I do not remember those people, outside." ³

Louis Adamic, in his book *From Many Lands*, interviews a prominent Jewish physician who says:

"I am supposed to be a fairly well-known doctor, but before I enter the home or hospital room of any of my influential or well-known or very wealthy Gentile patients, I look at myself in a mirror if I have the chance, to make sure about my appearance. If there is no mirror, I examine myself as well as I can without it. I feel my necktie to make sure it is straight. All this because I am a Jew. I am conscious that I am on trial; not only I, myself, but Jews . . ." ⁴

It is in experiences like these—rebuffs, slights, forbidden privileges and rights, rejections, and even physical danger—that many members of minority groups have their personalities molded. To find one's place in such a society often creates real difficulties.

Psychiatrists have called our attention to a type of neurosis they term "depersonalization." In this form of mental disturbance, the individual finds it difficult to establish relationships with other people. He is unable to feel any real warmth toward others; it seems to him that he is a soulless, mechanical being and he has no real sense of his own personality. The world and the people in it, including himself, seem to have neither reality nor rationality. Some of our modern novelists, notably Franz Kafka, have given us a real insight into this kind of emotion. Obviously, members of minority groups do not *all* develop this kind of personality disturbance. But the kinds of societal pressures they face tend to lower their self-esteem—a disturbing factor in healthy personality development.

In a volume called *The Mark of Oppression*,[5] two psychiatrists, Dr. Kardiner and Dr. Oversey, describe the result of an intensive study of twenty-five Negroes from varying socioeconomic backgrounds. One of their interesting findings was the fact that each of the individuals studied suffered from low self-esteem and a depreciated self-image. We cannot generalize unduly from such a small sample. However, additional psychiatric and sociological data indicate that the "mark of oppression" has pertinent relationship to personality development.

No two persons respond in identical fashion to the problems they face as minority group members. While it is certainly not true that minority group membership necessarily creates neuroses, there is increasing evidence that factors implicit in minority group membership can contribute to personality distortion. It is interesting to note here that research in the field of personality development indicates that basic and stable personality tends to develop early in life and seems to be highly correlated with a warm, loving, and secure family pattern. Many of our minority groups have a strong cultural tradition of the importance and value of family affection and solidarity. This family pattern frequently acts as a corrective or balance wheel for the personality formation of minority group children. It may account for the forbearance and fortitude with which many minority group members face the vicissitudes to which they are subjected.

The sociological concept of marginality is also helpful in understanding minority groups. Marginal members of society are those who find themselves accepted in some situations and rejected in others. They do not truly belong. They are never certain of their acceptance and consequently can never feel completely identified with the society in which they live.

Louis Adamic again gives us an excellent description of a young American of Japanese ancestry in just such a marginal status:

"That winter—1934–35—can't be laughed off easily. 'Nothin' doin'! Don't hire Japs! . . . Sorry we don't take on any Japanese! . . .' My feet still hurt when I think of all the wallowing I did up and down the hills of San Francisco. I was really frightened. Didn't I belong here at all? But, dammit, I was an American! If not, what was I? I was no 'Jap'! This is my country. I did belong! . . . Then there were times when my brain and feelings went numb. Occasionally a flash would come through the numbness. I've got to fight this thing out! But I could not shake off the dead mood. . . .

"When I started college, I had no definite plan. I was too young and green to try to blueprint my future; also too self-conscious and lacerated by my job-seeking adventures and resentful of my process of adjustment as a houseboy.

"I did not quite admit this to myself, but somewhere in me I knew that the world in which I was, was a mess so far as I was concerned, but no more so than I was a mess within myself. Very early in my sociology class I came upon the phrase 'marginal man,' which described me fully. I was neither here nor there; an orphan who was not an orphan, a 'Jap' who was not a 'Jap,' an American who was not really an American. When this occurred I told myself it was funny and laughed, but it also cut into me." [6]

Another important aspect of minority-majority group relations is the phenomenon of strong minority group identification as an adjustment to and a defense against majority group prejudice and opposition. Initially we may find a common tradition binding a group together, but in most cases where there is little majority group prejudice, the minority group gradually tends to merge into the majority group. In this country we have seen this process occurring with the Scandinavians and Germans, and it is happening with the Irish. Each of these groups suffered from the effects of prejudice, but as prejudice and discrimination fell away, the internal group cohesion began to disappear. For those minority groups against whom majority group pressure has been and remains great, strong group identification is extremely significant. It tends to give its members a feeling of security, aids them in organizing against discrimination, enables them to have in-group relationships, and creates a milieu in which they can be evaluated on their individual merits. Group identification in some instances leads toward prejudice against other groups by members of the minority group. It may provide a form of group-centricism that cuts its members off from the wider opportunities which they seek.

It should perhaps be mentioned here that group membership and group identification *per se* are characteristic of men in all parts of the world, in all points of time. Groups as culture carriers have been recognized and described since the dawn of history. In analyzing minority groups and their relationships to majority groups, we have called attention to the ways these group characteristics may become distorted in terms of our universally accepted democratic values and goals, and produce tensions and societal disharmony.

I have touched very superficially on prejudice, discrimination, and some aspects of minority group membership. In the past decade we have learned much about techniques for reducing prejudice, discrimination, and group tension. In this Institute series, however, we have tried to delineate and describe minority groups and some of the problems arising from minority group status. The *how* of reducing prejudice and discrimination was not our primary focus. Knowledge and understanding of minority groups are not, however, necessarily and completely divorced from social modification. New knowledge and new insights are frequently forerunners of the alteration of the status quo. Knowledge in itself cannot be equated with change; it is, however, frequently the prelude to change.

I should like to mention a few additional principles that are helpful in gaining insight into the understanding of minorities and, through this insight, reduce the barrier of communication between groups—perhaps the *sine qua non* in the reduction of intergroup tensions.

The first of these principles is adequate and accurate information about the peoples we are studying. What sorts of information? We need to know very concrete facts about their numbers, their age and sex distribution, their occupational and educational status, their birth and death rates, their housing and their health patterns. Each of these serves as a benchmark for comparing and relating minorities to other groups. Interestingly enough, although such data are readily obtainable, the extent of false and distorted information on these matters is astonishing. I am frequently surprised by the patent misinformation on these subjects quoted by many who are painstaking in ascertaining valid information in other areas of inquiry. Each of the essays has pointed out popular misconceptions about the groups they have discussed. It is trite to say we cannot understand a group about whom we have no information, or bits and pieces of misinformation. The cure for this is relatively simple. More valid information and increased education is needed to correct false concepts about the diverse groups that make up this nation and, indeed, those around the world.

The second significant thing we need to know about any group to further our understanding is what sociologists call the group's cultural roots. This calls for more complex study. Any people is in a great measure a product of its cultural heritage. The configuration of its history, tradition, attitudes, beliefs, family patterns and institutions, symbols and values, tend to give the group its uniqueness. A knowledge of this culture complex gives us some means of understanding its reaction to situations and out-groups.

Professor Thomas, in her paper on Japanese Americans, for example, described how many Nisei chose to remain in detention camps rather than be rehabilitated in the Midwest or East, because their strong tradition of family solidarity did not permit their breaking away from the family unit. Mr. Senior indicated that Puerto Ricans, often crowded together in inadequate housing facilities, would still welcome additional persons to their quarters because their kinship tradition requires that any relative, no matter how remote the connection is, is entitled to a home in the family dwelling. Professor Handlin pointed out that Jews traditionally have a sense of responsibility for members of their group who are less fortunate than themselves. These illustrations could be reproduced many times. They suggest how influential a cultural tradition may be in determining human behavior.

The knowledge of a group's culture complex has tremendous implications for adequate and satisfactory communication between groups. Obviously, we cannot communicate unless we have an adequate concept of what symbols are meaningful to a given group. We certainly cannot further understanding when we are unable to communicate. Social research has documented a myriad number of cases of group tension which arose through lack of basic communication between groups. This is true not alone in majority-

minority group relations; the same process has been observed in labor-management relations, in rural-urban tensions, and certainly we have abundant evidence of this fact in our international relations.

One of the real tasks that students of group behavior have is to learn to orient themselves in culture complexes that are not their own. Each of us reflects his own culture or sub-culture, and we tend to judge and evaluate behavior from our own framework and biases. One of the great contributions that anthropologists and sociologists have made to our understanding of groups lies in their detailed descriptions of the cultures and sub-cultures which form the accompaniment for the themes of the individual's behavior. By becoming aware of our own cultural forms and broadening our knowledge of other cultures, we take a step forward in the understanding of all groups of cultural diversity.

In summing up, I should like to reiterate that which has been implicit in my own paper and those of the previous writers. Essentially, many of the problems that arise in majority-minority group relations are not the result of differences but of the way we regard and react to these differences. The basic problem seems to be not diversity but the acceptance of diversity. Most thoughtful men recognize that group diversity is part of our world; how we learn to live with and accept diversity will determine in great measure the future of civilization as we have known it.

It is important to remember that honest disagreement is healthy and productive. It has been woven into the fabric of our own country almost from its inception. Uniformity has never been our basic creed, and we recognize the great contributions to both our material and spiritual way of life that various cultures have brought to us. We do not want differences to balk and paralyze the achieving of the goals we have all accepted. Nor can we reach these goals by demeaning and degrading individuals or groups who make up our society.

It is hoped that this group of papers in a small way has created an understanding of the meaning and scope of these problems. To the degree that it has aroused your interest in further pursuing the ideas we have brought to you, to that degree we will have achieved our aims.

I should like to close by quoting a letter of Thomas Jefferson's, written to his friend duPont in 1816, which sets forth his feeling about the Bill of Rights and which, like so many of his writings, seems so applicable today:

I believe . . . that morality, compassion, generosity, are innate elements of the human constitution; that there exists a right independent of force; that a right to property is founded in our natural wants, in the means with which we are endowed to satisfy these wants, and the right to what we acquire by those means without violating the similar rights of other sensible beings; that no one has a right to obstruct another, exercising his faculties innocently for the relief of sensibilities made a part of his nature; that justice is the fundamental law of society; that the majority, oppressing an individual, is guilty of a crime, abusing its strength, and by acting on the law of the strongest breaks up the foundations of society. . . .[7]

FOOTNOTES TO CHAPTER VIII

1. Louis Wirth, "The Problems of Minority Groups," in Ralph Linton, ed., *The Science of Man in the World Crisis*, p. 347, Columbia University Press, New York, 1945.

2. Arnold and Caroline Rose, *America Divided*, p. 14, Alfred Knopf, New York. 1948.

3. Lillian Smith, *Killers of the Dream*, pp. 218–219, W. W. Norton and Co., New York, 1949.

4. Louis Adamic, *From Many Lands*, p. 49, Harper and Brothers, New York, 1940.

5. Abram Kardiner and Lionel Oversey, *The Mark of Oppression: A Psychological Study of the American Negro*, W. W. Norton and Co., New York, 1951.

6. Louis Adamic, *From Many Lands*, pp. 203–205, Harper and Brothers, New York, 1939.

7. A. Whitney Griswold, "Thomas Jefferson: Anti-Totalitarian," in Edward N. Saveth, *Understanding the American Past*, p. 182, Little, Brown and Co., Boston, 1954.

Biographical Notes

on Contributors

JOHN COLLIER, formerly Commissioner of Indian Affairs of the United States, 1933–1945; at present emeritus professor of anthropology, College of the City of New York; president, Institute of Ethnic Affairs; author of: *The Indians of the Americas; Patterns and Ceremonials of the Indians of the Southwest.*

CORNELIS WILLEM DE KIEWIET, President, University of Rochester; chairman, Board of Directors, American Council of Learned Societies, 1953–1955; author of: *British Colonial Policy and the South African Republics; The Imperial Factor; A History of South Africa;* contributor to *The Constitution Reconsidered; Foreign Policy for the United States.*

JOSEPH B. GITTLER, professor and chairman of the department of sociology, University of Rochester; director, Center for the Study of Group Relations, University of Rochester; author of: *Social Thought Among the Early Greeks; Virginia's People; Social Dynamics; Your Neighbor, Near and Far.*

THEODORE H. HAAS, Chief, Indian Law Survey, Department of Justice, 1932–1939; Chief Counsel, Bureau of Indian Affairs, 1944–1950; author (with F. S. Cohen) of: *Handbook of Federal Indian Law.*

138

OSCAR HANDLIN, professor of history, Harvard University; editor of *The New England Quarterly;* winner of the Pulitzer Prize in history for *The Uprooted;* winner of the Dunning Prize of the American Historical Association for *Boston's Immigrants;* also author of: *Commonwealth; This Was America.*

FATHER JOHN LA FARGE, S.J., associate editor of *America;* director, National Catholic Rural Life Conference; author of: *Interracial Justice; The Jesuits in Modern Times; The Race Question and the Negro; The Manner is Ordinary.*

WAYNE A. R. LEYS, professor of philosophy and dean of the graduate division, Roosevelt University; author of: *Ethics for Policy Decisions; Ethics and Social Policy.*

IRA DE A. REID, professor of sociology, Haverford College; former president, Eastern Sociological Society; author of: *The Culture of Racial and Ethnic Populations; The Urban Community; The Urban Negro Worker.*

CLARENCE SENIOR, research associate, Bureau of Applied Social Research, Columbia University; director, Social Science Research Center, University of Puerto Rico, 1945–1948; author of: *Puerto Rican Emigration; The Puerto Rican in New York City; The Puerto Rican Journey.*

DOROTHY SWAINE THOMAS, professor of sociology, University of Pennsylvania; former president, American Sociological Society; director, Evaluation and Resettlement Study of Japanese Americans; author of: *The Spoilage; The Salvage.*